How to capture thinking, convey information and collaborate using visuals

Express Edition

Lynne Cazaly

First published in 2013

www.lynnecazaly.com

National Library of Australia Cataloguing-in-Publication entry:
Author: Lynne Cazaly, 1964 -
Title: Visual Mojo: How to capture thinking, convey information and collaborate using visuals
ISBN : 9780987462916
Subjects: Visual thinking.
Creativity.
Communication.

Illustrations and layout by Lynne Cazaly

Cover design by Lliam Amor

VISUAL MOJO

How to capture thinking, convey information and collaborate using visuals

Express Edition

Lynne Cazaly

OOH, THIS PAGE IS BLANK.
PERFECT FOR SOME OF YOUR VISUAL MOJO...

CONTENTS

Oh no, why did the mojo go? ... 6
Make meaning from complexity ... 9
Use Visual Mojo to make good…awesome ... 16
Let's get it started: where are you at now? ... 26
Tools of a trade ... 31
The skills of Visual Mojo ... 34
Let's do some lines ... 35
Shapes ... 42
Writing ... 52
Bullets and lists ... 60
Borders ... 62
The visuals of Visual Mojo ... 64
Visual Mojo 60 Quick Pics ... 79
Play the Quick Pics sketch game ... 141
Putting it all together ... 147
Listening to capture ... 148
Where are you at now? ... 151
Next steps – what to do now? ... 155
About the Author ... 167

OH NO, WHY DID THE MOJO GO?

You may remember being told by an art teacher, a parent, a school 'friend' or someone else in your earlier years that drawing, art, sketching or painting wasn't your strong suit.

The look, muffled laugh, hand gesture or eye roll that accompanied those words may have encouraged you to focus more on words than pictures in the years since then.

I think we've all got a little carried away using our extensive vocabulary that we've lost our Visual Mojo – our confidence, interest and capability to quickly sketch or visualize things.

The power of a visual to help tell our story is not in question - apparently a picture paints a thousand words.

I passed some chalk drawings on the street last week. They probably weren't drawn by an adult. Grown-ups hardly ever squat on the pavement with a handful of chalk and tell stories with pictures!

Drawing in public must be right up there with dying, speaking in public, looking at spiders or snakes, scaling heights and other scary stuff.

It can be terrifying to put our thinking out there. And not just in words but in pictures! Cue sweaty palms for even the most creative thinkers and smart operators.

Where did our mojo go? When did we decide to stop using pictures and instead use oh-so many words?

Using this little book you'll soon have your Visual Mojo again.

If you're not in to drawing or feel a little artistically challenged, that's ok. It's about your thinking, your ideas, communicating well with others and the conversations you have with real human beings.

Focus on all of that more and think less about the drawing part of it.

Lynne Cazaly in Drawing Class at ten years of age. True story. Shattered!

Simplicity
is the
ULTIMATE
Sophistication

- Leonardo Da Vinci

MAKE MEANING FROM COMPLEXITY

There is so much information. We have so little time. We have such a capable brain.

Yet we're not making the best use of our brain's incredible filing cabinet.

Leonardo Da Vinci said 'Simplicity is the ultimate sophistication'.

Unfortunately, sometimes we seem to act as if 'complexity is the ultimate way of trying to appear smart'.

Do we think that the more complex it looks and sounds the smarter we'll appear?

Or, the more complicated we make our message, the less people will question us perhaps?

But with a fire hose of information blasting us in the face daily (did I hear someone call it a 'fur ball of complexity' stuck in our throats) how do we make meaning of it all?

Our ancestors used cave art and hieroglyphs to capture, convey and collaborate.

What have we done?

We have just a few seconds to get our message across.

We've got to get our Visual Mojo back and quick!

ONE CLICK AND TANGLED CAN *LOOK* PERFECT

We all got a bit caught up in the Microsoft Word of it all!

Perfect boxes, straight lines and 'click to insert' a clinically precise object or chart.

Too easy.

But not so engaging and interesting after awhile, particularly if the thinking behind it is still tangled up.

Quick and perfect is so last century.

Pictures and technology can do some wonderful work together, make no mistake. The problem happens when we use the technology and perfect shapes as a smoke screen for confused content or tangled thinking.

You know some awesome stuff. And you think some wonderful ideas and things.

At some point, most days, we need other people to understand what we know and what we think.

That is communication.

We send them a message or information, they receive it and they confirm back to you that they've got what you said. Not just received it, but understood it too.

Punching out a few words, inserting a few shapes and pressing 'print' doesn't always lead to clarity.

It might look straight, clean and all lined up, but it could contain a load of marsupial droppings.

Getting your Visual Mojo back will help in your communication with others. It can help you **untangle thinking**. It can help you **get things straight …** and then you can **make something of it.**

Mmmmm clarity, can't you just taste it?

Visual Mojo will help you untangle thinking, get things straight and make something of it. Mmmm tasty.

HAND-CRAFTED THINGS ARE IT

Hand-crafted beer.

Hand-made bread.

Made-by-a-deeply-passionate-person jewelry.

Limited editions.

Personally signed.

Just for you.

So many hand-crafted, made with love, tailored just for you things are enjoying resurgence in this post-industrialised era. If we're moving beyond the information era too, where are we? Some say the era of knowledge or meaning and making sense of all of that complexity.

Maybe it's the era of getting back to being a human. Living in the moment, being present, mindful and being authentic.

Have you seen all of those cool RSA Animate videos (yes, go Google!), the sketch videos of one person drawing and writing as another person speaks? There's a resurgence and interest in visual thinking, and careers like graphic recording and visual facilitating are now earning people a good living. It's a great living when you're helping people understand each other.

There are tasty restaurant and café menus with hand sketched lettering and pictures of leafy salads and steaming cups of coffee.

Hand-made is human-made.

It's creating a stronger connection. It's delivering a clearer message.

Bring some human, hand-made love to what you're thinking, talking about, selling and pitching.

People will be captivated. If it was thought about by a human, then why not communicate it like a human?

A great gift of love – made by a human, given to a human, from another human.

DON'T GO COLD TURKEY ON WORDS

Visual Mojo, visual thinking, graphic recording, sketchnoting - whatever you want to call these visual things, they have a common thread; they involve words and pictures, or words and images or words and symbols. It's the 'and', the 'also', and the 'as well as'.

But keep using words.

Don't go cold turkey and drop words ok?

Pictures alone won't get the job done. Words are still an important partner in communication and thinking.

It's not picture charades. Imagine if it were…

> *"Hey guess what I think the strategy of this team should be? I sketched it here."*
>
> *"Ummm, well it looks like a giraffe and a lama had a baby and then we're going to plant trees."*
>
> *"Wrong! Guess again."*
>
> *"We give up. Literally."*

The 'I can't draw' paradigm was born for many people in their earlier years. I think we also picked up the (less than helpful) belief that you have to write everything down.

I remember learning dictation at school. The purpose of dictation was to test that you wrote down everything the teacher said. Everything. And that it was spelled correctly, punctuated appropriately and all captured good and proper.

Many grown-ups I consult to, train and coach still think they have to write everything down! It could be about butt-covering too, in case questions are asked or accusations are made. But even then, visuals can come to the rescue and give you great recall, reference and detail.

Keep using words – in fact, when you put visuals to work, you can use fewer words than you do now.

No need to play picture charades. Keep using words.

USE VISUAL MOJO TO MAKE GOOD... AWESOME

Visuals and words help people communicate quicker and more clearly and can help you create awesome when you're working with others. Here's how to make good stuff greater:

Capture

Use Visual Mojo to collect, capture or catch conversations, discussions, ideas and thoughts. Whether these are your own thoughts and ideas or those of others, Visual Mojo is captivating, engaging and memorable.

Graphic recorders are people who do great capture standing at the front, side or back of a group event, listening and representing the key points using Visual Mojo. What a wonderful summary and artifact from what may be a complex and meandering conversation!

You can use Visual Mojo to capture at conferences, workshops, seminars, school classes, presentations or brainstorming sessions.

Convey

Pull the plug on PowerPoint (or at least hit 'B' on the keyboard and the screen will go to black) and communicate your key points and messages using visuals. You'll be more engaging and it will really make you think about what YOU need to communicate to THEM.

Visual Mojo is impactful when you're conveying information in meetings, presentations, pitches, sales conversations and speeches. Turn off clinical and hi-fi; turn on human and low-fi.

Collaborate

When people get together to talk, discuss, decide, ponder, problem solve or create, Visual Mojo is at its best. Generate ideas, solutions and possibilities. Don't let the thinking, exchanges and conversations vanish into thin air; collaborate with others and 'see' what you're all thinking, 'see' what's possible and 'see' where you're heading.

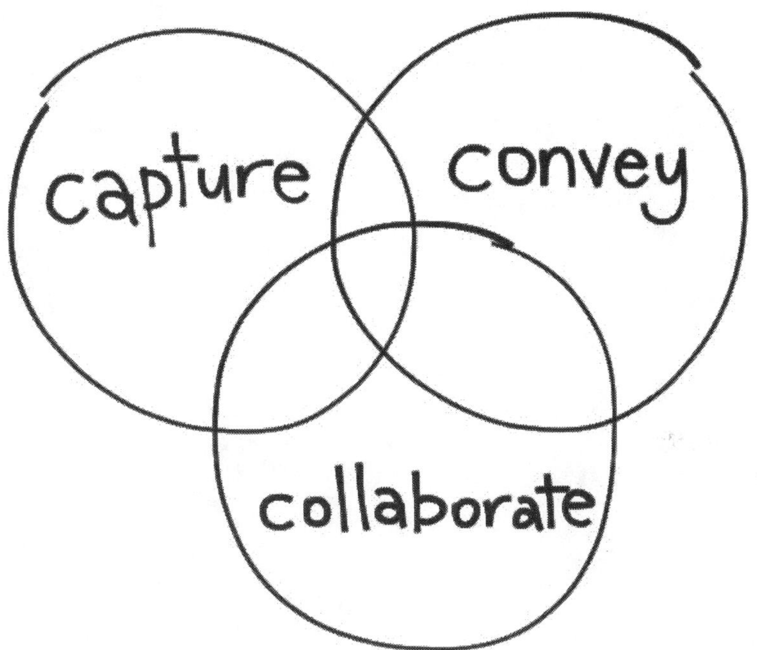

Visual Mojo – everyday ways to make communicating things quicker, clearer, cleaner

SO...WHAT COULD YOU CAPTURE?

I like to listen. I have learned a great deal from listening carefully. Most people never listen.

- Ernest Hemingway

QUESTIONS

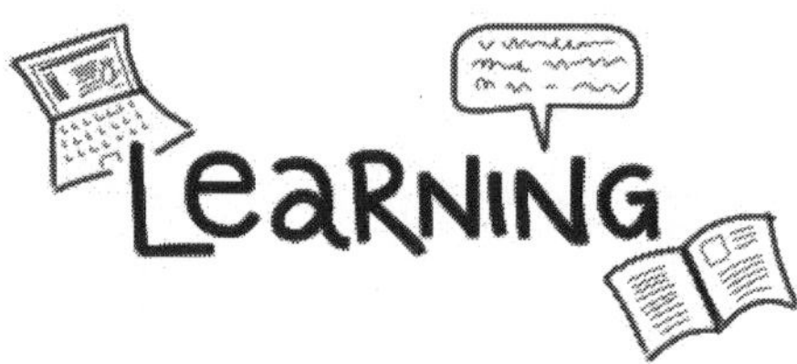

FEEDBACK

WHAT COULD YOU CONVEY?

I passionately believe that's it's not just what you say that counts, it's also how you say it - that the success of your argument critically depends on your manner of presenting it.

- Alain de Botton

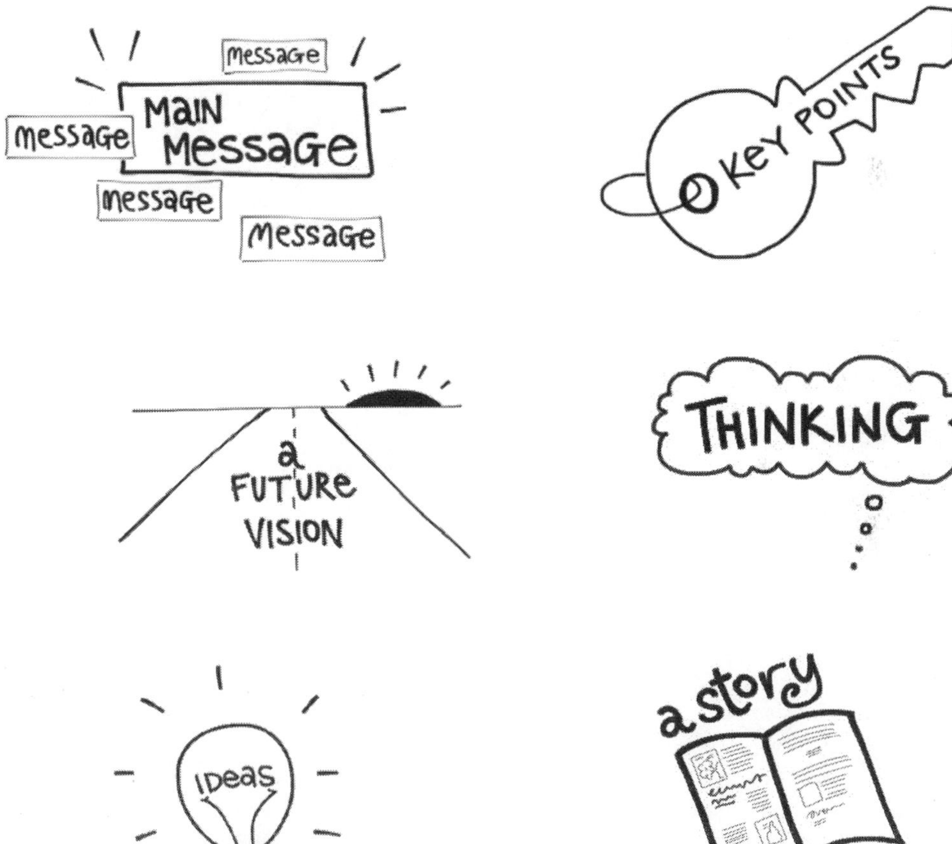

HOW COULD YOU COLLABORATE?

Alone we can do so little; together we can do so much.

- Helen Keller

Map out a
PROCESS

PROBLEM
SOLVING

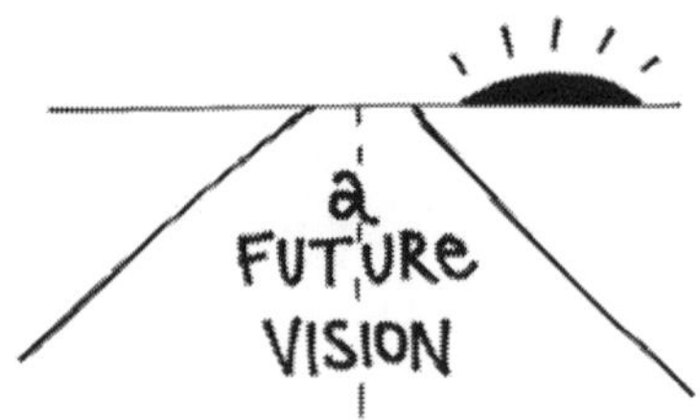

DOODLE ABOUT IT...

WHAT COULD YOU CAPTURE, CONVEY AND COLLABORATE?

A small visual anchor can hold a weight of information

– Lynne Cazaly

OOH LA LA – IS THIS HOW YOU COULD USE IT?

There are lots of ways to use Visual Mojo. Here's one…

Laurel, a participant in one of my two day Visual Mojo courses came along on day two and said she had been having a few troubles helping her young school-aged son Ben memorise and remember a French poem for homework.

"Homework can often end up being a warzone; he has to do it, sometimes I can't help him out and next thing we're in a stand-off," explained Laurel.

After learning the skills of Visual Mojo on the first day of the workshop (just as they are in this book) Laurel took the skills home and put them to work to help Ben out.

"We really collaborated and we created a small visual anchor to accompany each of the eight lines in the poem," she said. "We sketched out what each line of the poem was about."

In just a few minutes – not hours, minutes – Ben was able to recall each line of the poem.

"Ben's confidence took off in an upward direction," said Laurel. "He was so pleased he was able to remember them in the right order and with greater accuracy than stumbling about with them just the day before."

And yes, perhaps some of his earlier learning had helped embed the poetry and the visual anchors were an added tool.

But Laurel was thrilled, Ben was on a high and together they'd created a solution to a challenging homework task, quickly and clearly.

As Ben's confidence grew with the content and with his memory giving him the visual reminders he needed, he was able to focus on his accent, pronunciation and delivery.

"This was one homework task that was a joy," said Laurel.

Voila!

REAL LIFE PEOPLE SAID THIS...

Here's what real life people said about the power of Visual Mojo – once they'd learned the same skills that are contained in this book you're holding!

Engaging People – Keeping people interested

"It makes you realise that we write a lot of unnecessary 'words' in meetings. This approach to communication makes you listen for valid key points and document them."

"A more effective way of capturing key points of planning discussions with businesses - more engaging."

"We need to be more creative and innovative in our approach to communication … this is an excellent mechanism to get creativity into the system!"

"There is better recall of the information discussed at a meeting or conversation. The visuals capture more of the essence of the discussion and they have more use to participants even after the session."

"Visual thinking for a business is a unique experience that allows people to express themselves in a creative way. Not only does it allow a team to have a fun and interactive working session, but it creates some great visuals to utilise in the business."

The Way I Work

"Capturing information in meetings, learning sessions or different group formats is more visual and engaging."

"Useful tool in the kit bag for anyone acting as trainer, speaker, leader, consultant, teacher, communicator, facilitator."

"I'll be using more flip charts and whiteboards in workshops and meetings. Also the flipcharts are more interesting, more impactful."

"The way I draw a flip chart in a meeting or workshop has changed. I've already had a participant want to take my flip charts home."

Putting it in to Practice

"I have used some of the learnings in two phone hook ups and a meeting so far. I tidied up the notes and I can now understand my notes!"

"No more 'what's that word, what did I mean when I wrote that' and no more filing it away to never be used, referenced or shared."

"Have used it already and it turned something that was a mess (too many cooks in the kitchen) into something that I can map out and we can all agree to!"

"Less text, more visuals drawn in real-time when facilitating, learning and analysis and design with groups."

"Think visual first when preparing any communications I plan to integrate it into every piece of work."

"Your own drawing capability is very unique and your drawings are only as good as how you view them yourself. Each drawing of mine clearly had its own unique DNA."

My Confidence

"I thought going in 'that I'm not really good at drawing – I never took art' so I wondered if this would be a problem, but I overcame that. I feel more confident now to put some pictures on my notes!"

"I can't draw so well but I can now see how different and simple shapes and lines, shading and layout can make such a difference."

"I now have much greater confidence in replacing boring narrative and words with symbols and pictures and labels."

"It gives me more skills that I can use to challenge how I and others think about how we deliver information."

"Yes I have more confidence in my capacity to use this approach to note taking and facilitation."

"I feel that my confidence and capability had shifted to another level. I have Visual Mojo!!"

LET'S GET IT STARTED: WHERE ARE YOU AT NOW?

Yes, let's get it started and kick off with getting the 'capture' part of Visual Mojo sorted.

I think if you can **capture** information or ideas with visuals and words, you can make the transition over to **conveying** information and then **collaborating** with others.

Let's see where you're at right now with taking notes, capturing information and listening to thinking. Then at the end of Visual Mojo, you'll see how far you've come.

In a moment, you'll begin capturing information. Yee ha! But first, let's get something to capture…

I love love love listening to TED talks. These are the 'technology education design' talks delivered by experts all around the world.

Go to **www.ted.com** and pick yourself a fairly brief talk to listen to, say five minutes or less. An alternative to TED is to listen to an interview on the radio or television, or to listen to a meeting, conversation or discussion.

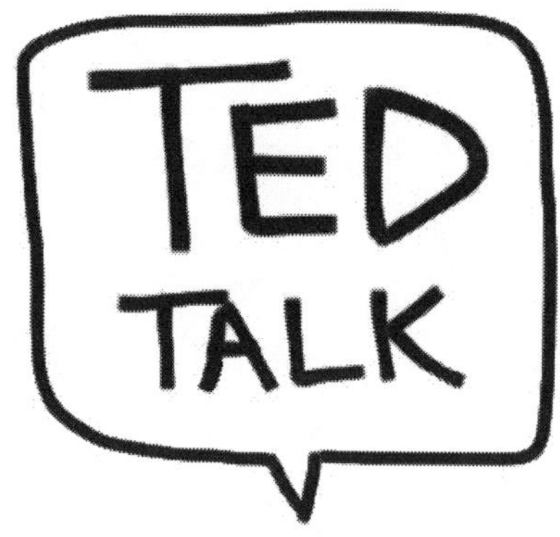

There's no need to do anything fancy, just do what you normally do when you're listening to information or a presentation, and write notes as you usually would.

Are you ready?

Pick up a pen, press play on the TED talk or interview and write your notes for the talk on the next three pages over there… yes, write in this book, this is your Visual Mojo book!

THIS IS WHERE I'M AT NOW...

THIS IS WHERE I'M AT NOW...

THIS IS WHERE I'M AT NOW...

REVIEW... REFLECT

So how did it go… the **capture** part of Visual Mojo?

- ☐ Are you all words and nothing else?
- ☐ Is it written in a linear style, straight down-the-page?
- ☐ Do you write in more of a mind map approach – starting in the centre and radiating out?
- ☐ Did you use any lines or arrows?
- ☐ Are there any boxes or triangles or circle shapes?
- ☐ Did the page end up blank because you were listening so hard?
- ☐ Are there any random shapes among the words?
- ☐ Are you already using a few images, symbols or icons?
- ☐ Did you go crazy and play picture charades using all pictures?
- ☐ Are you not sure what you'd call it… but you'd like some Visual Mojo - quick?

Whatever approach you currently use to capture information, we won't change it completely.

We'll adjust and add to it to make it awesome.

So you can continue to use this approach of adding some new things to your existing style – and keep doing this to build on and develop your Visual Mojo.

Take your time through Visual Mojo and you'll be adding some icons, visuals and symbols to your notes for the next time you **capture** information, ideas and thinking.

Remember, using visuals with key words and points will make the information easier to remember, more engaging to look at and read, and the process of listening can be more enjoyable.

TOOLS OF A TRADE

A few notes for you on the tools of the trade of visual notes and flip charts… visual thinking… Visual Mojo.

A pen and a piece of paper is a great start. You need no more.

But if you want more, want to discover and create more and try different materials and textures, consider these…

- [ ] Pencils
- [ ] Pens
- [ ] Markers
- [ ] Pastels
- [ ] Chalk
- [ ] Gel pens
- [ ] … your choice

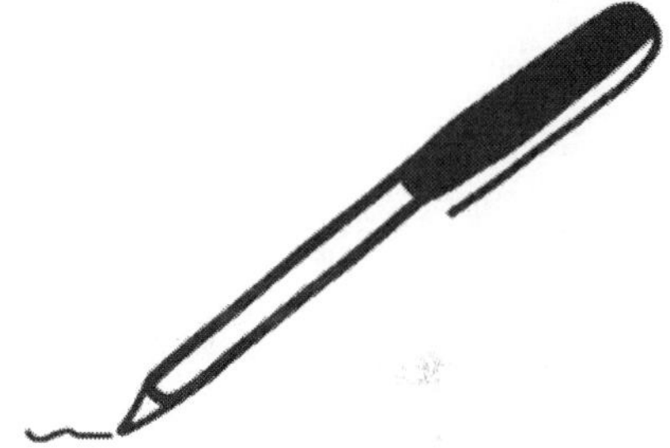

FLIP CHARTS AND WHITEBOARDS

So many meeting rooms, venues and workplaces have whiteboards bolted to the wall or flip chart stands hiding in storage cupboards.

Bring them out of hiding and have them close at hand. They're going to get some action!

SKETCHBOOKS AND JOURNALS

Visual journals and notebooks come in all sorts of sizes: from A6 to A5, A4, A3, A2 and the larger A1 and A0. Whatever size paper you find best to work with, have it on hand. I look out for sketchbooks in news stores, arts suppliers and stationery haunts.

IPADS AND TABLETS

Many of the visuals in this book Visual Mojo I created using the iPad and the app 'Brushes'… oh, and my finger as the stylus.

There are lots and lots and lots of drawing apps to try out if you like the digital approach to Visual Mojo. I love them because they can always be on hand, they're easy and oh-so flexible for work and play.

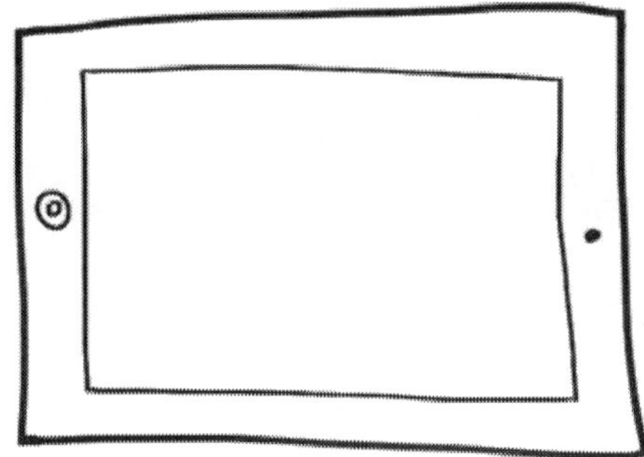

OOOPS! WHITEOUT AND LABELS

When I'm training or speaking on visualization, so many people ask "But what if you make a mistake?"

A must in your little bag of tricks is some 'whiteout' liquid.

If you're using paper, you can cover the error quickly with whiteout. Then when it dries, apply a label, like a mailing label you'd put on an envelope or a white sticker. The white smooth surface gets you back to the base texture of paper – but only if you're using paper; stickers don't look so good on the iPad screen!

If you're using an iPad or tablet, hit the 'undo' button. It's a winner! If you don't have an 'undo' feature on the app you're using, select a thick white brush tool and simply cover over or erase your slip up.

Gone! Now move on… nothing to see here!

THE SKILLS OF VISUAL MOJO

Now let's get started on the skills and techniques of Visual Mojo.

If you can power through the next 40 pages, you'll have the know-how to be getting your Visual Mojo back.

We'll start easy and keep on building up … just like we do in one of my workshop sessions.

So get yourself some tools of the trade and get ready to go get your mojo!

LET'S DO SOME LINES – DROP LINES

They may seem pretty simple, but lines and strokes on the page are at the very foundation of Visual Mojo. There are three main types…

Here is where you let the pen or marker sweep down the page or drop down the page, quickly. Keep the pen moving swiftly. Quick lines are straighter!

HORIZON LINES

Horizontal lines across the page can be drawn swiftly too. Drag the pen quickly across the page – from left to right or right to left.

THROW LINES

Diagonal lines from top to bottom or bottom to top, left or right are throw lines. It's like you're throwing the pen across the page. Keep it moving quickly. No need to keep it all neat and perfect; it's the handcrafted effect that will make your Visual Mojo look good, real, engaging.

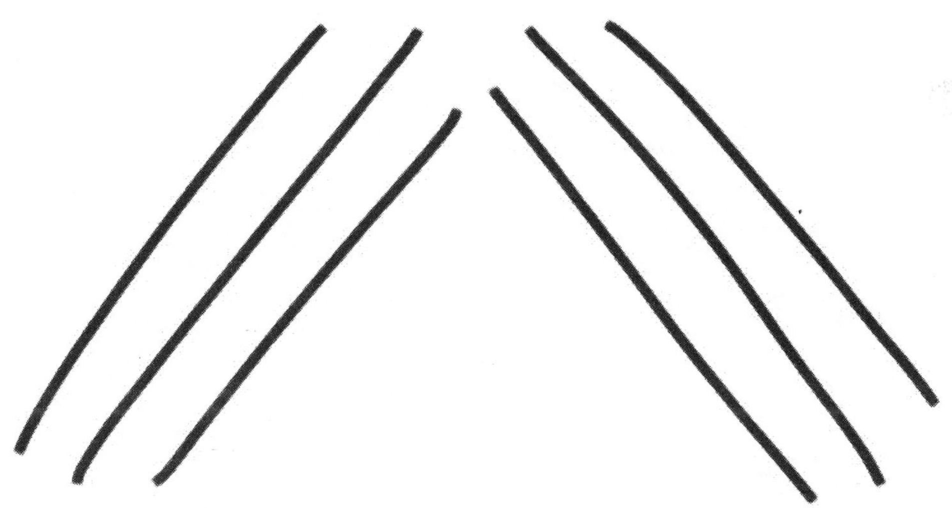

SHORTEN IT

Now shorten those drop, horizon and throw lines to just a few inches or centimetres in length.

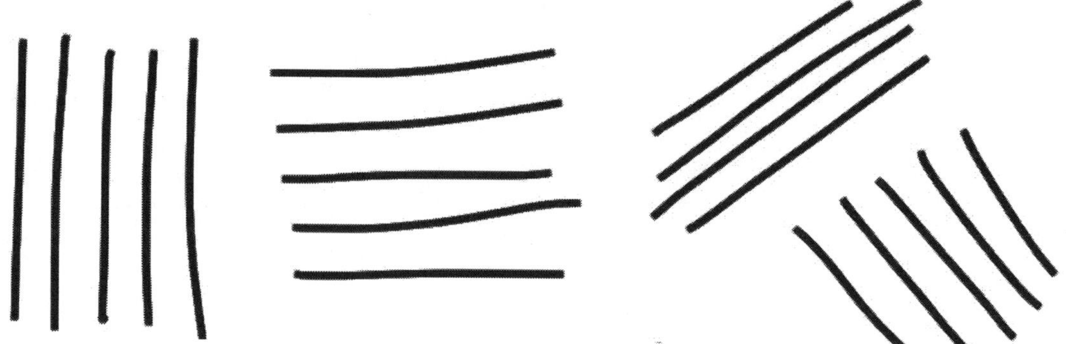

TOGETHER THEY ARE THE MATRIX

Using those lines, you can quickly create a matrix, table or grid.

How many columns wide, how many rows across? You choose.

Quickly sketch out a grid or matrix here.

Lines coming together like this are a handy tool to capture or present information or use as a graph or chart.

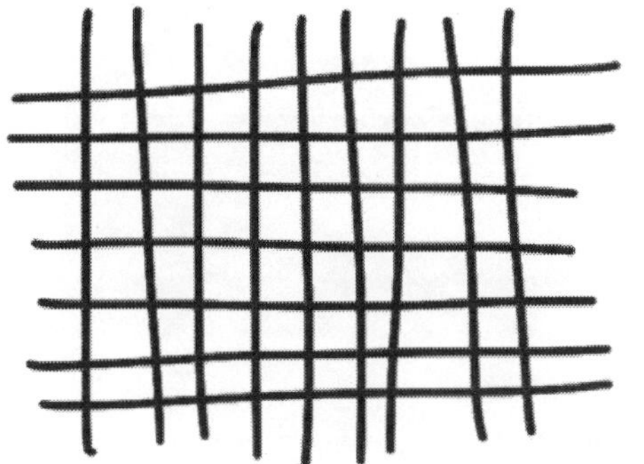

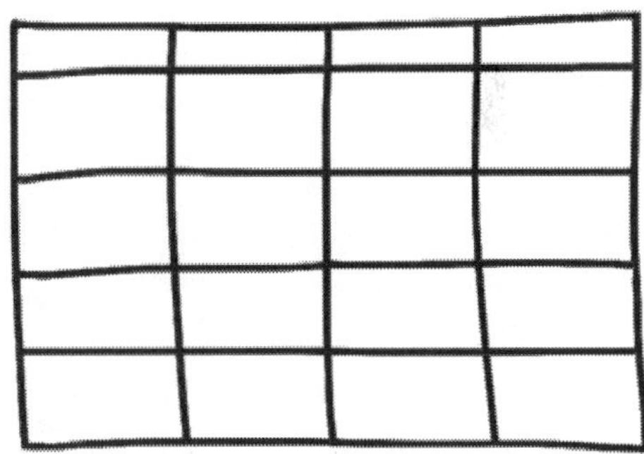

WIGGLE IT, JUST A LITTLE BIT

Try wobbly, wavy and wiggly lines, swirling lines and scribbly lines

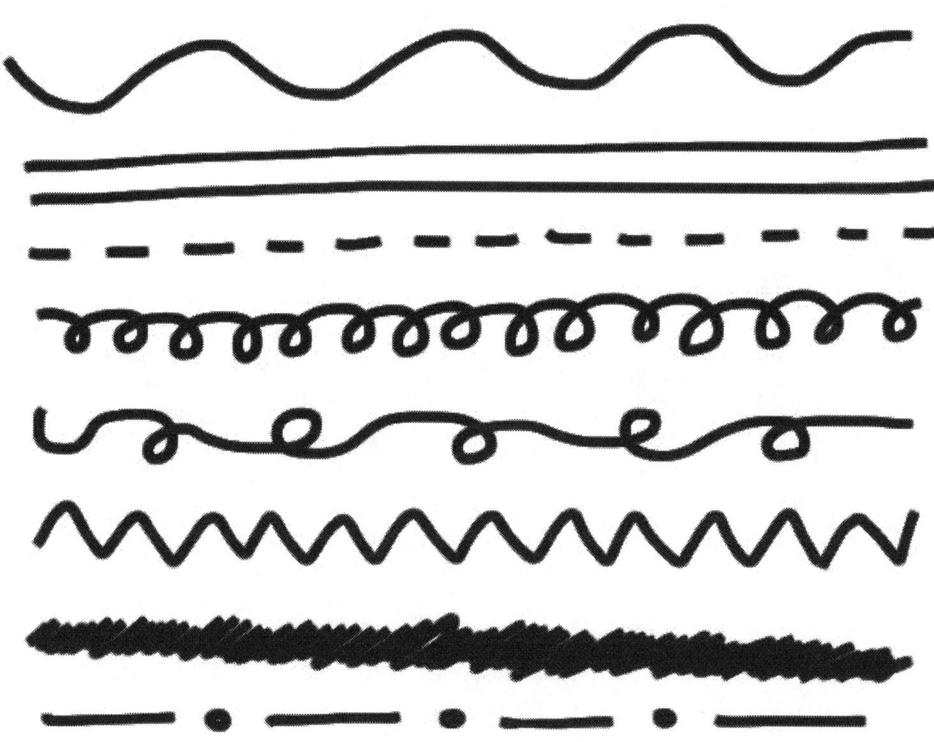

PRACTICE SOME LINES...

SHAPES

Many an artist, architect or designer will say that that the world is made up of things in the shapes of circles, squares and triangles. You can see buildings as squares or oblongs; the tops of trees as circles; cars as squares with circles for wheels; people as triangles (broader at the shoulders, narrower at the feet) and a circle on top.

CIRCLES

Circles and ovals can represent concepts like community, unity, oneness, holistic, process, circular, cycles, round, curving, full circle, running around in circles…

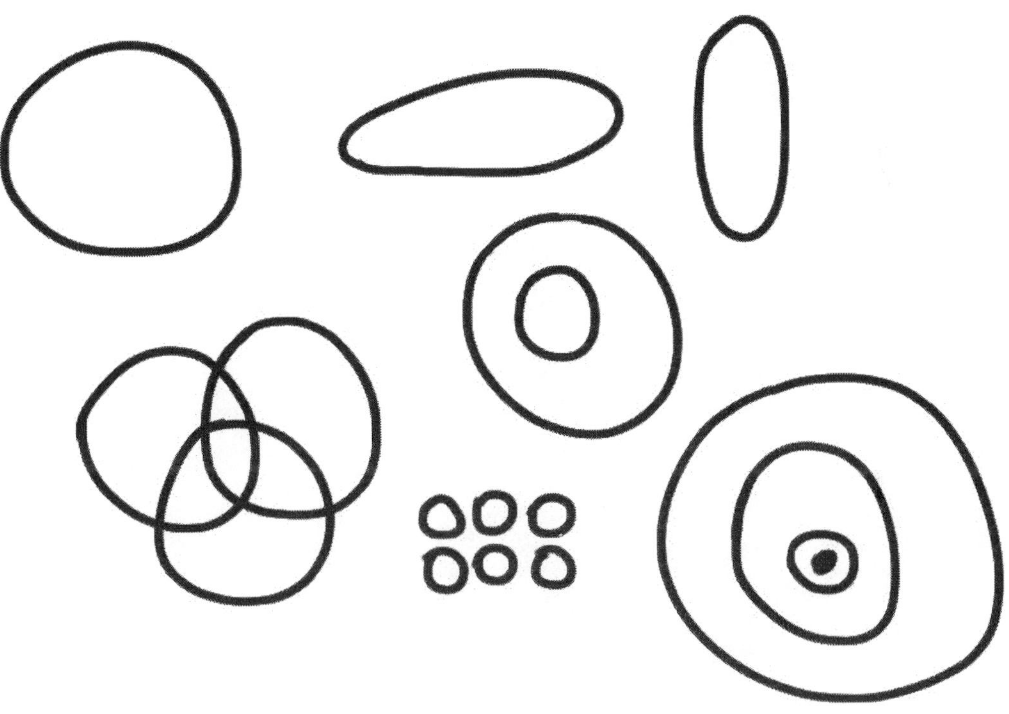

DRAW SOME CIRCLES...

SQUARES

Squares and oblongs are more structured. They can represent things that are defined, organized, methodical, constructed. You can use squares to 'put things straight' and to section things off or to show pieces and chunks.

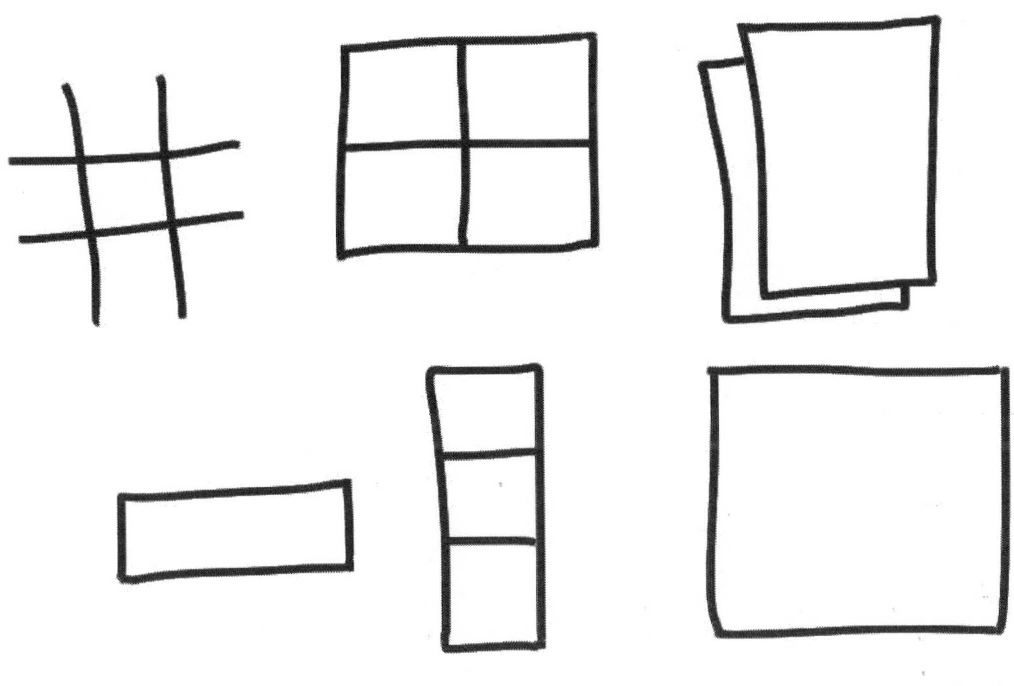

DRAW SOME SQUARES...

TRIANGLES

Triangles have three sides so they're great to represent concepts that have three points or components. Triangles can also represent growth, evolution, progress and advancing through different levels or stages. Triangles can point too!

DRAW SOME TRIANGLES...

ODD SHAPES & BLOBS

For all the other times, when things aren't a circle, square or triangle… you can use 'the blob'. Any shape. With sharp edges, straight edges or round corners. Any odd shape is a good shape.

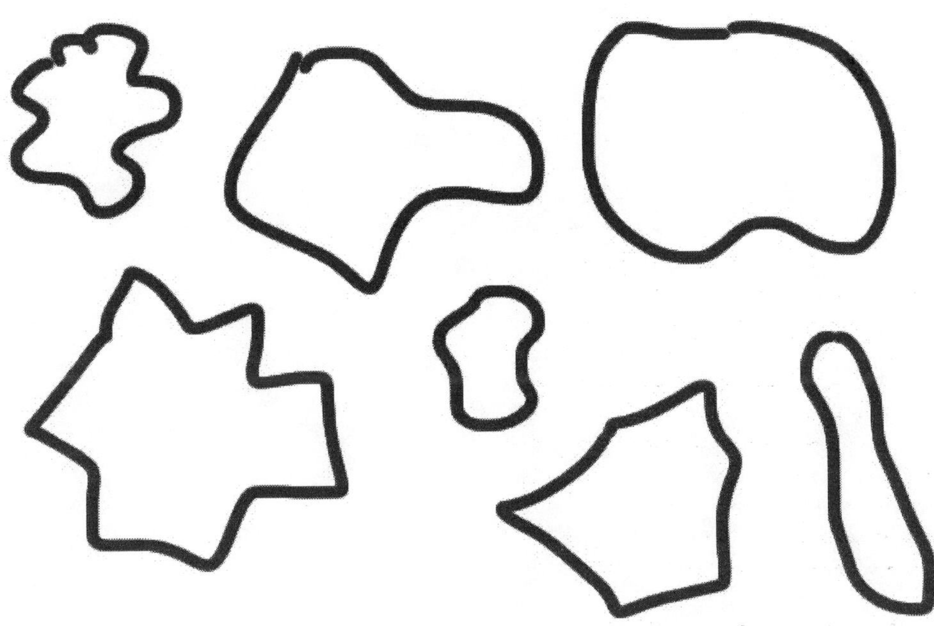

DRAW SOME ODD SHAPES & BLOBS

ARROWS

Arrows point. They show process, direction, relationship, impact, effect or flow. Arr – oh! Draw some lines and shapes and put arrows on and around them.

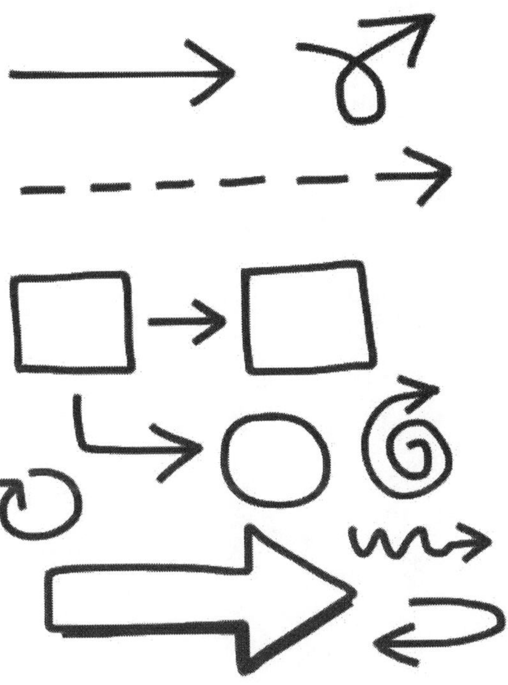

WRITING

Yes, writing! With Visual Mojo, visual notes and visual thinking, there is still some writing involved. It's not all about pictures. Words continue to play an important part in the capture, convey, collaborate process.

So let's have a look at your writing here...

CAPITALS/UPPER CASE

Write out the capital or upper case letters of the alphabet below:

A B C

CAPITALS/UPPER CASE

Go again with the upper case alphabet. Aim to do it faster, keep it level, and keep the form, clarity and shape of the letters.

A B C D E F G H I J K L M N O P
Q R S T U V W X Y Z

PRACTICE MORE CAPITALS/UPPER CASE

A B C

LOWER CASE WRITING

Now try some lower case writing.

abcdefghijklmnopqrstuvwxyz

PRACTICE MORE LOWER CASE WRITING

Go again. Aim to do it faster, keep it level, and keep the form, clarity and shape of the letters. Don't let the letters touch, but rather 'nestle-in' next to each other.

NUMBERS

Practice the numbers 0 - 9 here:

0 1 2 3 4 5 6 7 8 9

FAMILIAR WORDS

Write out some of the words you deal with regularly in your work, learning or personal interests e.g. leadership, success, manager, creative, painting, design, garden, project, team, environment …

Practice writing these, scattered around the page. Then given them a shape or border.

Project

Leadership

Team

Design

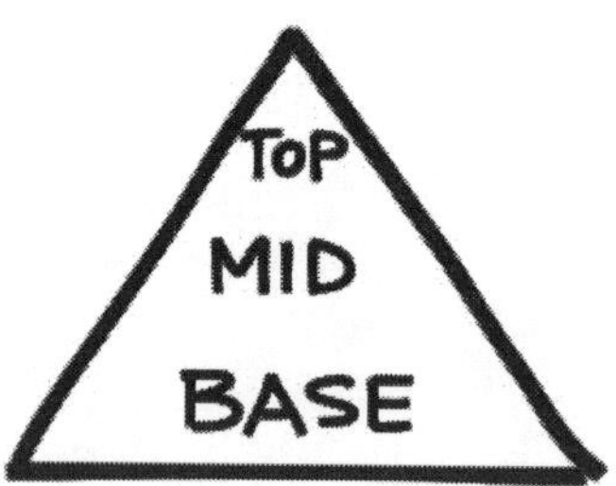

WRITE SOME FAMILIAR WORDS + SHAPES

BULLETS & LISTS

One of the quickest ways to use Visual Mojo is to make your writing look easier and clearer to read. Using a list of key points or 'bullets' can help.

You can use the shapes we've already learned as bullets for the dot points…

CREATE SOME MORE BULLETS FOR LISTS

BORDERS

Borders give focus to words, pages, concepts and visuals.

They draw you in. They train your eye to the important stuff.

Remember the lines we did earlier?

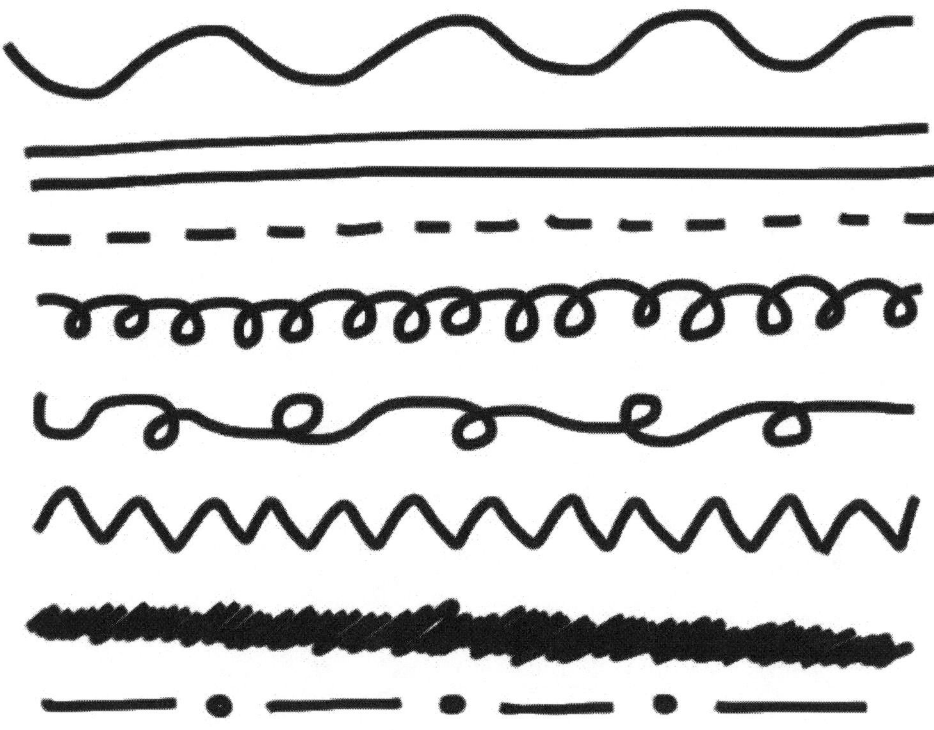

CREATE SOME BORDERS AROUND THIS PAGE

THE VISUALS OF VISUAL MOJO

We've got lines, shapes, writing and lists sorted out – let's get even more visual with visuals. That's icons, symbols, illustrations, pictures… things, people, places, objects.

PEOPLE

Being able to quickly draw people is one of the best skills in Visual Mojo. That's because people are connected to almost everything we do. If it isn't about you, it will be about them, us, me, her, him and those people over there.

It will involve that team, the department over there, the business in that next town, the users and customers, stakeholders, the public, the local community, patients, clients, students, shareholders, the media.

They are all about people. Even when they're groups, they're still groups of people.

You've got to be able to draw people so you can clearly capture, convey and collaborate with Visual Mojo.

You'll want to communicate with people, engage and influence people, listen to people, reach out to people, share with people and make things happen with people.

So get you're marker ready…we're gonna do 'people'!

IT'S TIME FOR THE STICK FIGURE TO 'GROW UP'

Does this little stick figure look familiar? It may be similar to how you would draw a person now … or how you drew people when you were a child.

But for Visual Mojo, I think the stick figure needs to 'grow up'.

Sure, stick figures are a quick way to draw people, but there's at least one other quick way to draw people and the end result looks a lot more elegant and human.

5 STEPS 'PENGUIN' PEOPLE

I call them '5 Steps Penguin People' because I know in five short steps they will be drawn (and they do have a sort of penguin look about them – even though they look more human. Huh? What? Human… penguin!)

The five steps go like this: head, arms, legs, feet, face. Done!

MAKING PEOPLE THE STAR

Another style is the 'star person' – made up of the points of a star. These can look even MORE human!

Start with an oval or circle for the head… draw four points of a star as the arms and legs. Then you can close in the points of the star to make them look even more like arms and legs. Or you can leave them pointing out and they look like they're leaping.

I always put feet and faces on star people!

A PAGE FOR PENGUIN PEOPLE AND STAR PEOPLE

Try different sized heads, arms, legs, feet and face. You'll see how different they can look… and you'll begin to find your own style.

CLOUDS

Cloud shapes with scalloped and curved edges can make for great Visual Mojo. They are lovely shapes or borders for text and words. They can represent thoughts or thinking bubbles too.

DRAW SOME CLOUDS HERE...

SPEECH BUBBLES

Just as cloud shapes can represent thoughts, speech bubbles can capture quotes, feedback or comments.

The speech bubble can be any shape at all! And now you know how to draw people, you can draw these cool speech bubbles or thought bubbles next to people!

Here's how: write the words first (that you want enclosed in the bubble) and then draw the pointy arrow. Then choose whatever shape you like. Draw the shape from one side of the pointy arrow, right around to the other side.

TRY OUT SOME SPEECH BUBBLES HERE...

BANNERS

When you've got something big and important to capture in Visual Mojo, like a heading or a title… why not use a banner. They look pretty clever AND they're quite easy to draw.

1. Write the words, then draw a box around them.

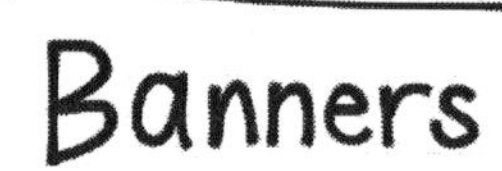

2. Next put a sideways 'w' or 'm' on each side of the box. Make sure the bottom line of the 'm' or 'w' keeps going a little way under the box.

3. Join the 'm' or 'w' lines up to the box.

4. Put in the diagonal line that shows the banner is 'folding' back on itself.

PRACTICE SOME BANNERS

BOOKS AND DOCUMENTS

Paper, books, newspapers, magazines, documents, reports, envelopes, journals – all of these paper things can easily be sketched with square shapes and lines. Look!

PRACTICE SOME BOOKS AND DOCUMENTS

LIGHT GLOBES

The light globe is THE icon! I think it's one of the greatest things to sketch because you can use it to represent so many concepts. Things like innovation, creativity, a bright idea, thinking, marketing, big ideas, brainstorming… can all be represented with a light bulb or light globe.

I think if you can quickly sketch a light globe, you've got an impressive looking icon that is portable, practical and flexible.

Put little emphasis marks spraying out around the globe to show that it's 'on'.

SWITCH ON SOME LIGHT GLOBES HERE

VISUAL MOJO

60

QUICK PICS

QUICK PICS

When many people are in the process of getting their Visual Mojo back, they're keen to get some examples of the visual icons, images or symbols they can use.

It's fine to have a bunch of icons on hand, but they're no help if you haven't practiced sketching them and ready to use them.

So here in **Visual Mojo Quick Pics** you get both: 60 visual icons AND somewhere to play around and sketch them out!

The illustrations aren't meant to be neat and perfect with precise lines and corners. Oh no! Quick Pics are supposed to be fast, simple, easy … yet clear.

If you think 'yeah, nice, but how could I use a picture of a coat hanger?'… I've included a few words with each illustration to suggest just that! There are ideas for what the visual could represent, what it could communicate, how you could use it. (By the way, I often use a visual of a coat hanger to represent: structure, framework, arrange, closet, coat, clothing, retail, pricing).

So pick up that marker, pen or pencil and have a play and practice with **Visual Mojo Quick Pics.**

You can practice them in the spaces provided.

Keep adding to your own library of Quick Pics so you can boost your communication effectiveness. There is space to do that at the end of these **60 Visual Mojo Quick Pics**.

If a picture tells a thousand words, this library of simple illustrations can tell thousands and thousands…

COMPASS

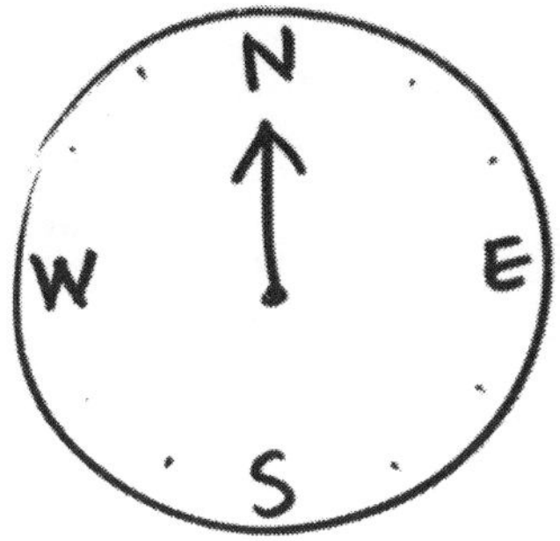

IT CAN MEAN...

Direction

Goal

Progress

Planning

Focus

PRACTICE SKETCHING IT HERE

TREE

Growth

Family

'Money Tree'

Harvesting

Environment

ROAD SIGN

Curves Ahead

Speed Bumps

Direction

Plan

BOMB

Ticking Time Bomb

Issue

Crisis

Problem

Serious Risk

LADDER

Progress

Step by Step

Process

Plan of Action

GLASS

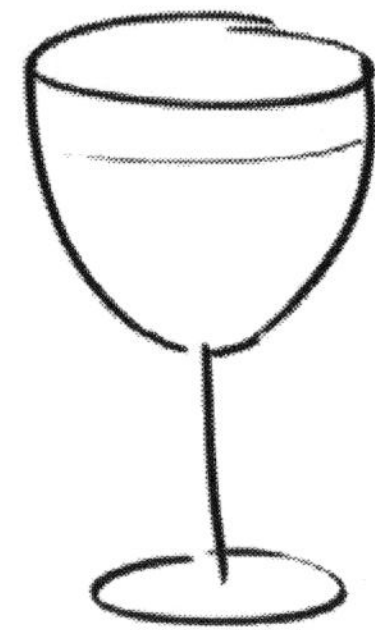

Celebration

End of Day

Cheers

Glass Half Full

HEART

BRICK WALL

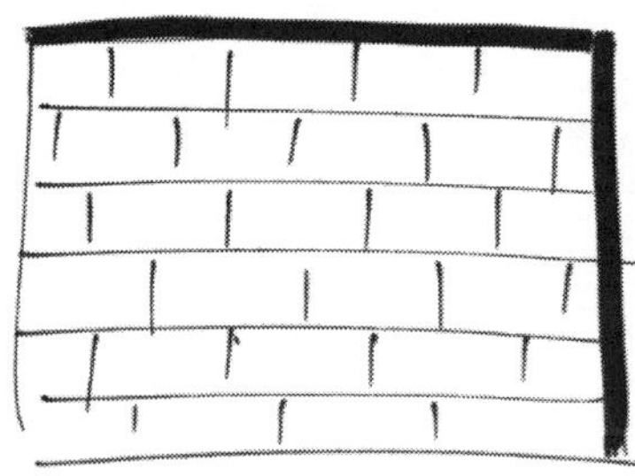

Barrier

Obstacle

Resistance

Obstruction

Stuck

FLOWER

Growth

Beauty

Thank you

Alive

Youth

WORLD GLOBE

World

Global

International

Regional

Environment

BOOK / PUBLICATION

Report

Magazine

Newspaper

Media

Publications

OPEN BOOK

Report

Document

Newspaper

Media

Story/Storytelling

PAGES

Letter
Email
Survey
Report
Strategy
Plan

MONEY

Finance

Budget

Expenditure

Resources

Cost

CHECK BOXES

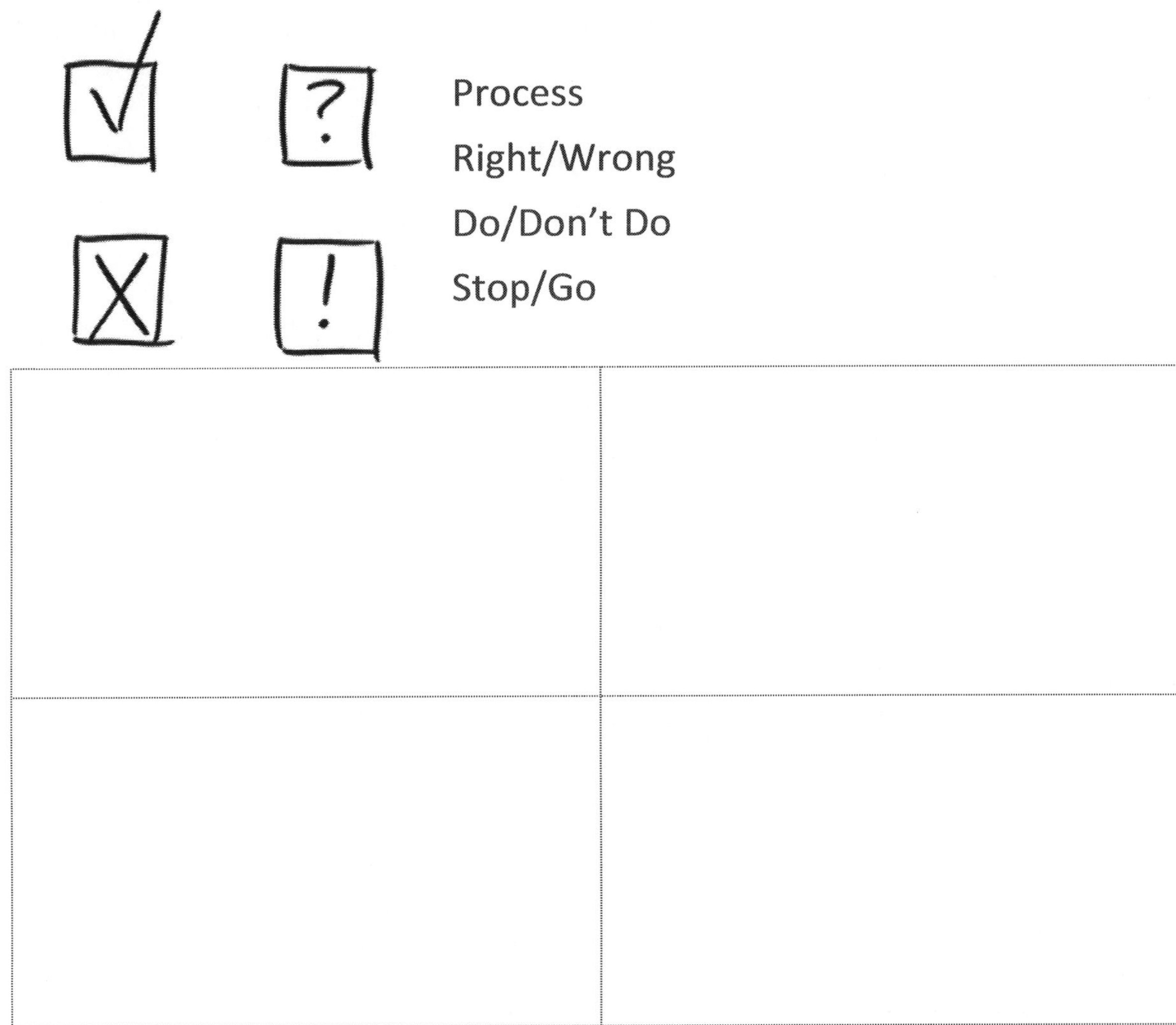

CLOUD

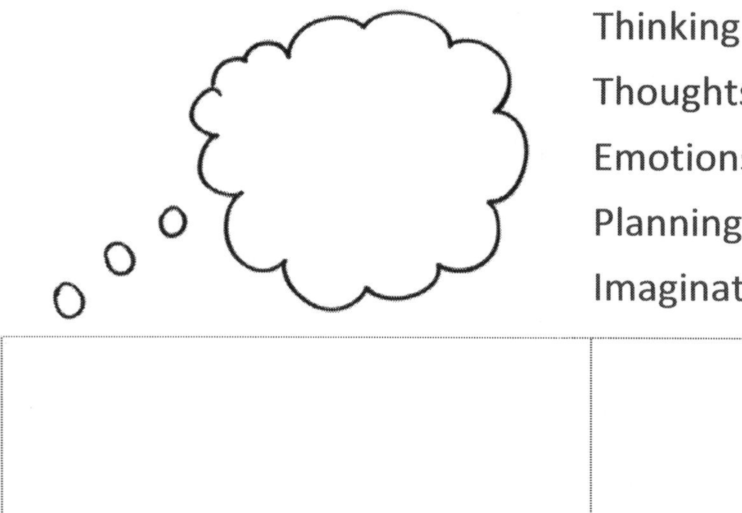

Thinking

Thoughts

Emotions

Planning Ahead

Imagination

BANNER

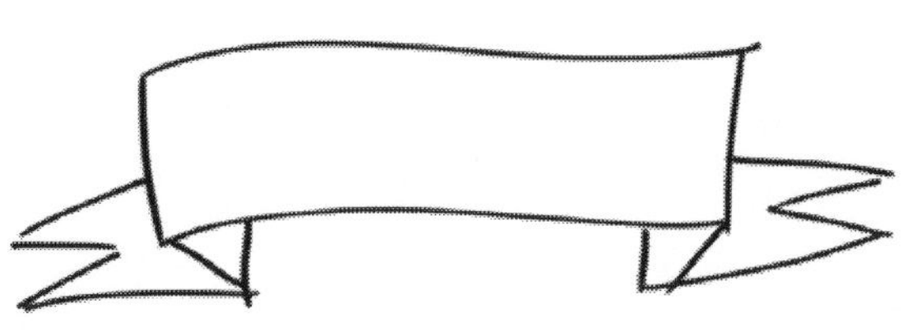

A Heading or Title

Success

Start/Finish

Celebration

Congratulations

FLAG

Red Flag
Attention
Risk
International
Celebration
Sign

FLIP CHART

Training

Sign

Announcement

Presentation

Advertising

PERSON

Customer
Leader
Manager
Staff
Stakeholder
Individual

PERSON + PRESENTATION

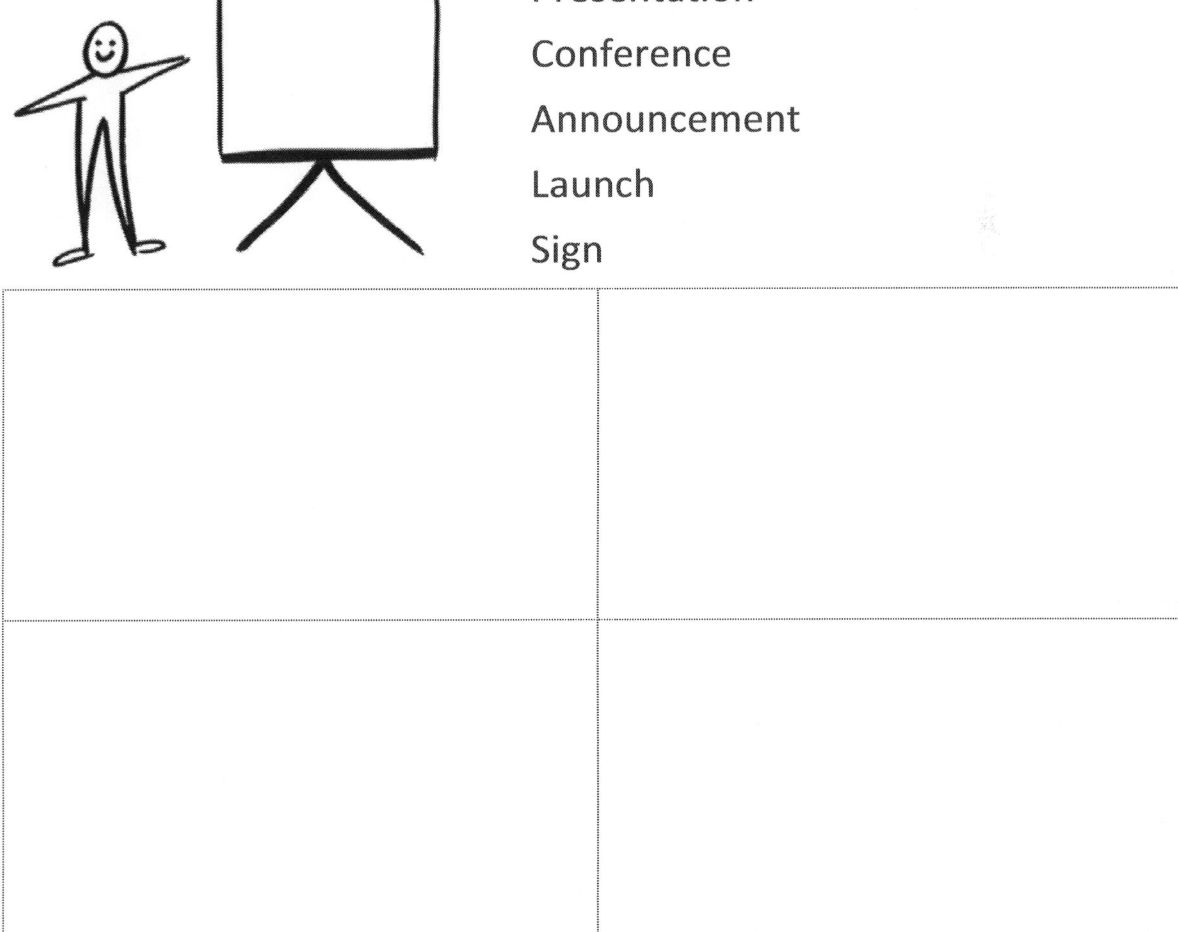

Presentation

Conference

Announcement

Launch

Sign

GRAPH

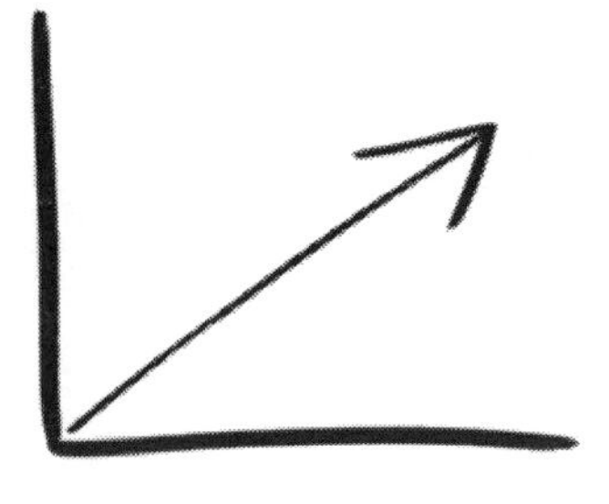

Growth
Direction
Sales
Finance
Results
Success

ORGANISATION CHART

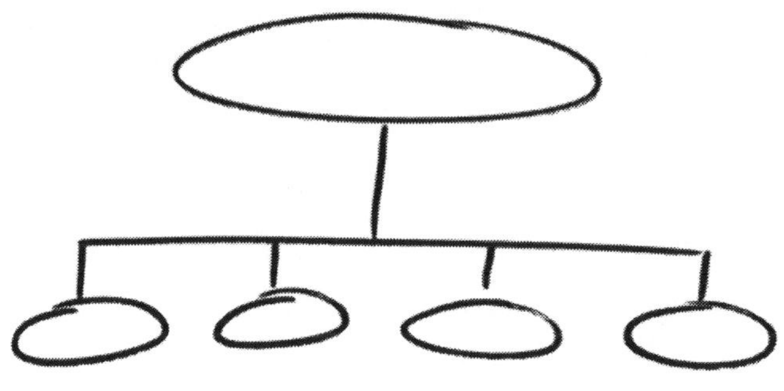

Business

Restructure

Leadership

Management

Functional Roles

SHAPES

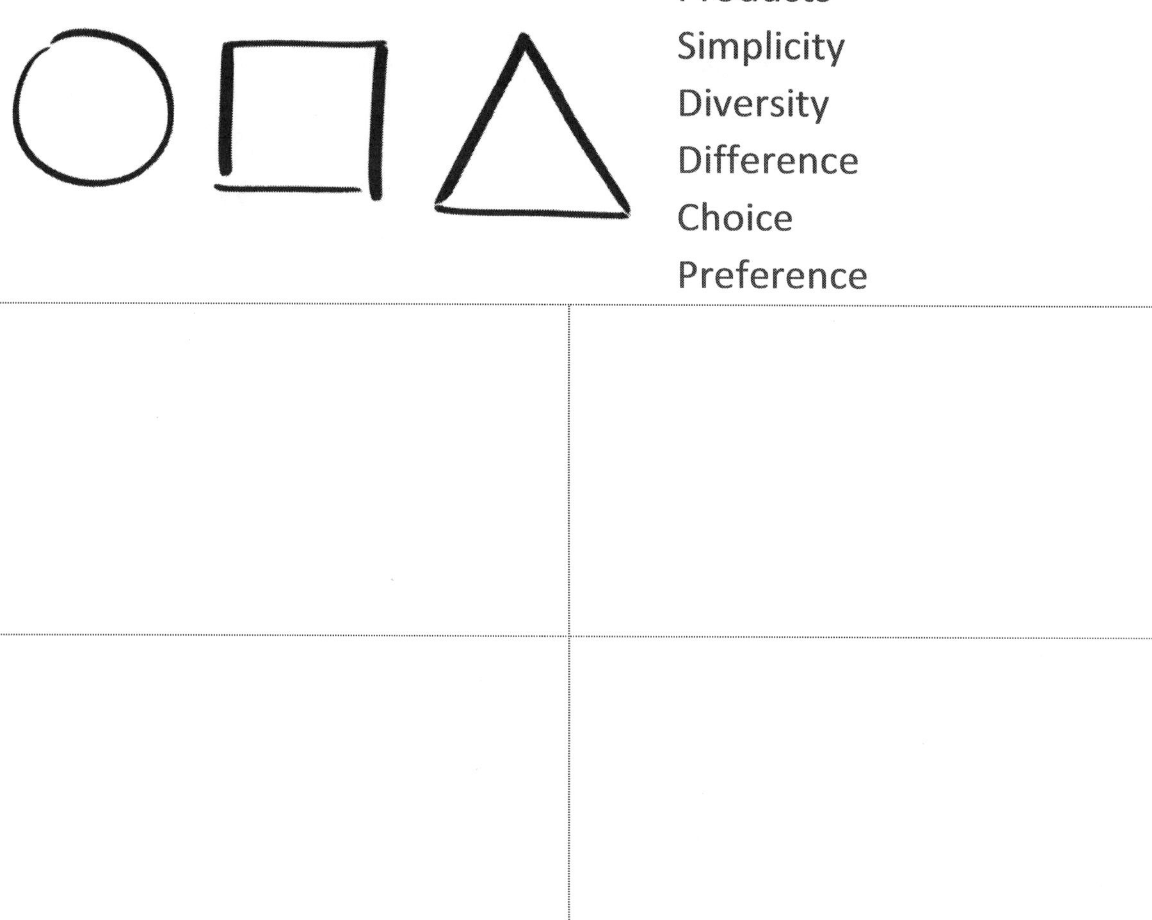

Products
Simplicity
Diversity
Difference
Choice
Preference

TARGET

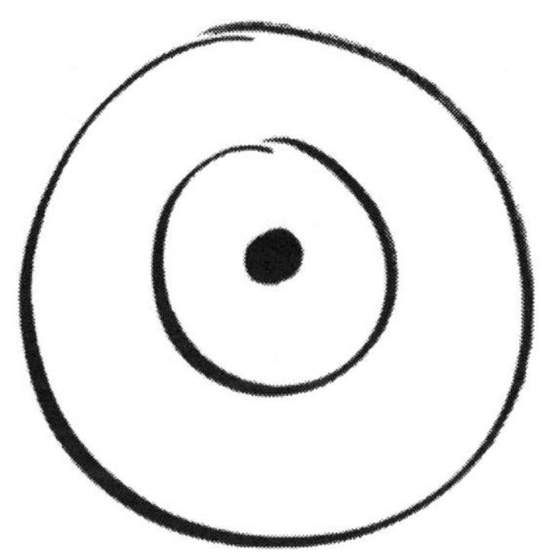

Goal

Bullseye

Outcome

Target Market

Focus

ROAD

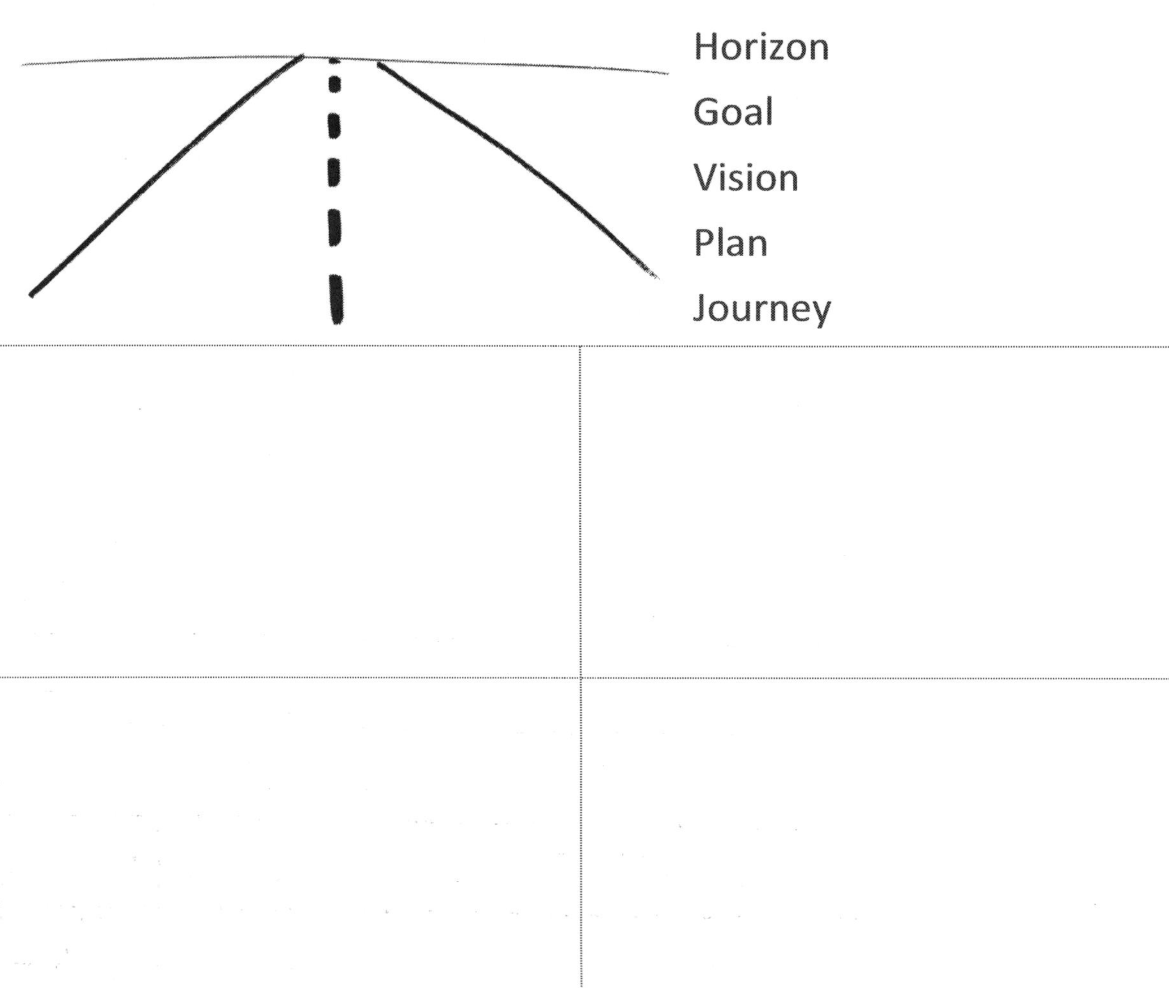

CURVY ROAD

Journey

Uncertainty

Plan

Steps

Strategy

ARROW

From Here to There

Change

Plan

Strategy

Direction

Outcome

BLOCK ARROW

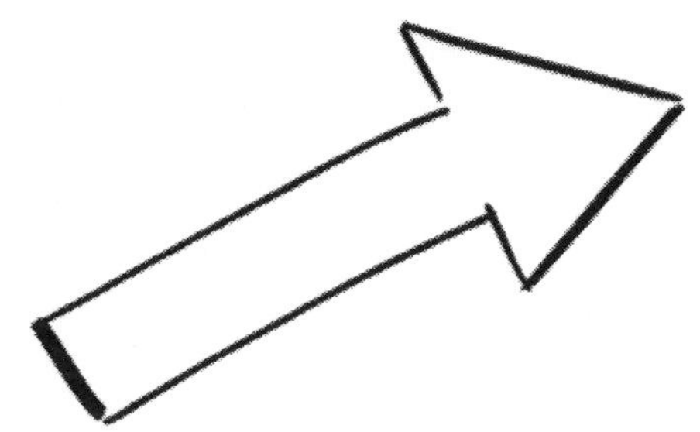

Direction
Vision
Goal
Change
Sign
Success

LIGHT GLOBE

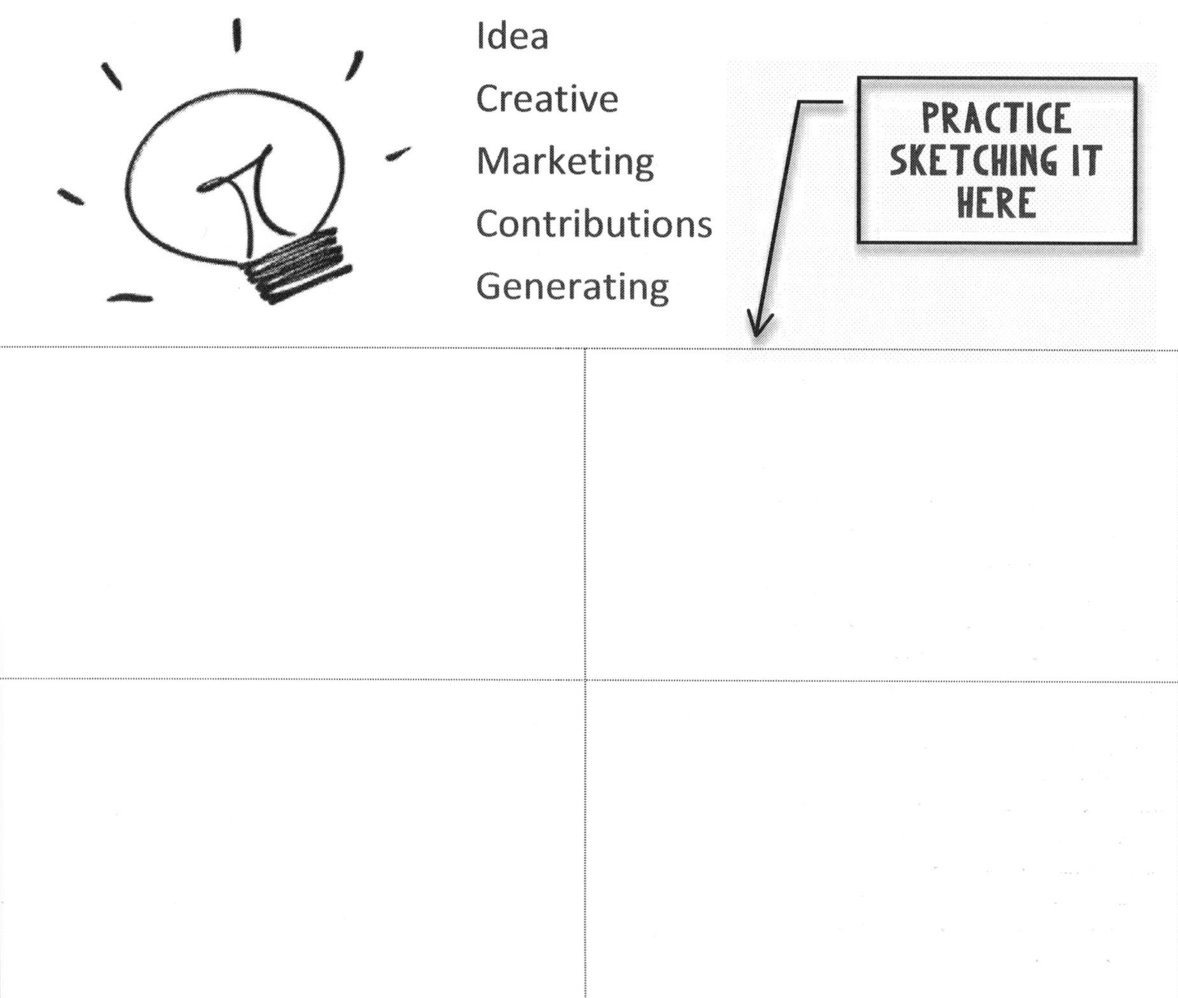

Idea
Creative
Marketing
Contributions
Generating

PALM TREE

Growth

Holiday

Lush & Tropical

Relax

Shelter

BELT

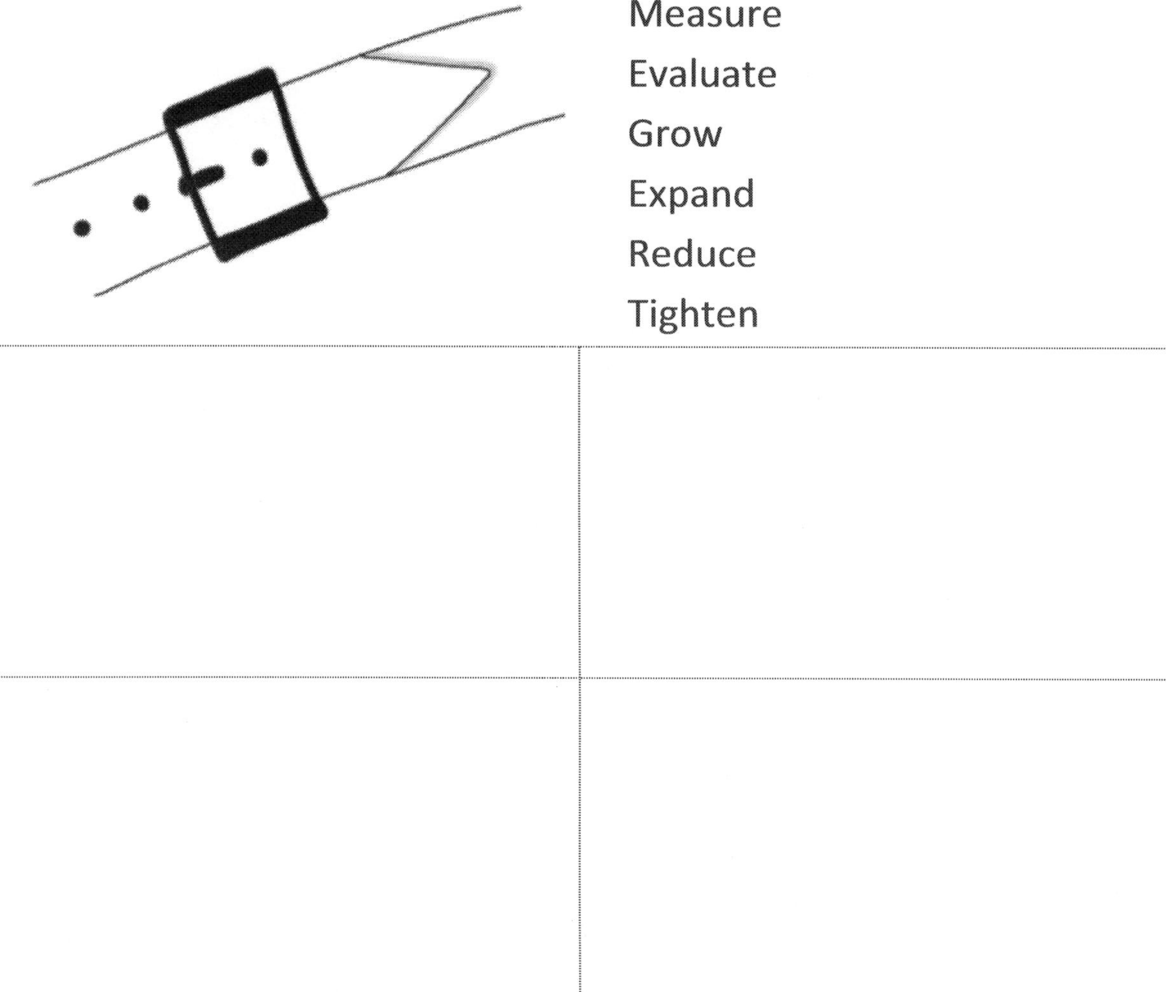

Measure
Evaluate
Grow
Expand
Reduce
Tighten

START BANNER

IT CAN MEAN...

START

Start

Beginning

Journey

Race

Adventure

CAMERA

Snapshot
Picture
View
Panorama
Landscape
Perspective

FOCUS

Focus

Attention

Pinpoint

Spotlight

Emphasis

SPEECH BUBBLE

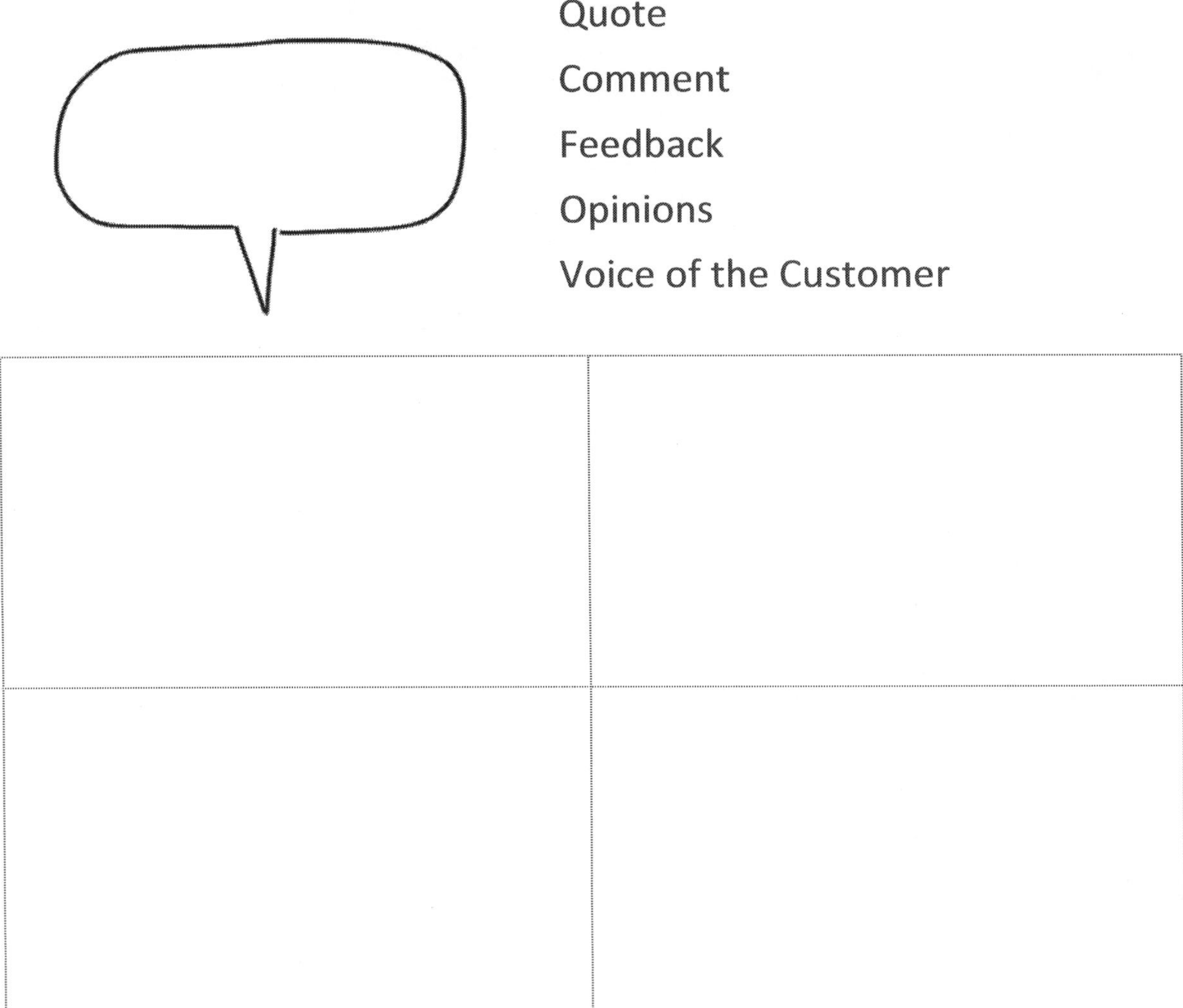

Quote

Comment

Feedback

Opinions

Voice of the Customer

T-SHIRT

Marketing

Brand

Message

Merchandise

Clothing

BAG OF GOODS

Manufacture

End Product

Goods

Raw Materials

Marketplace

DRINK

Glass
Thirst
Half Full/Half Empty
Retail
Service
Customer Needs

BUCKET

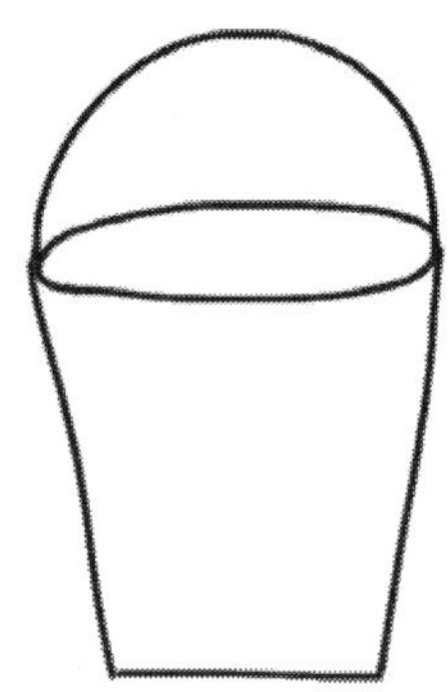

Collect

Fill

Full

Leaking/Leaky

Bucket List

TAG

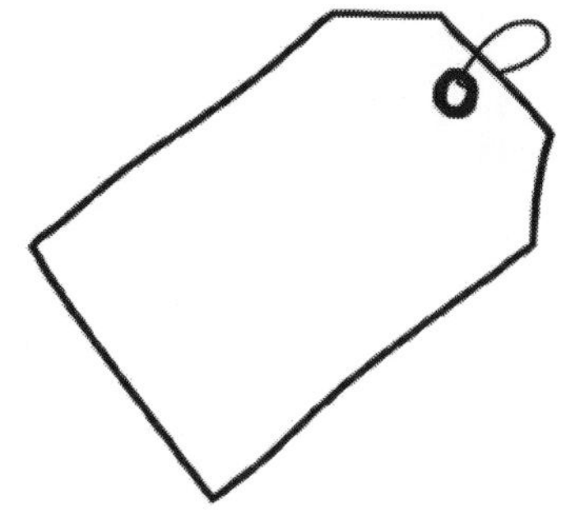

Price
Value
Amount
Sale
Special
Announcement

ENVELOPE

Email

Communication

Distribution

Delivery

Fulfill

FESTIVE SEASON

Decoration
Gift
Prize
Celebration
Box
Giving

TRAFFIC LIGHTS

Go / Stop / Slow
Wait
Checkpoint
Beware
Control
Manage

FENCE

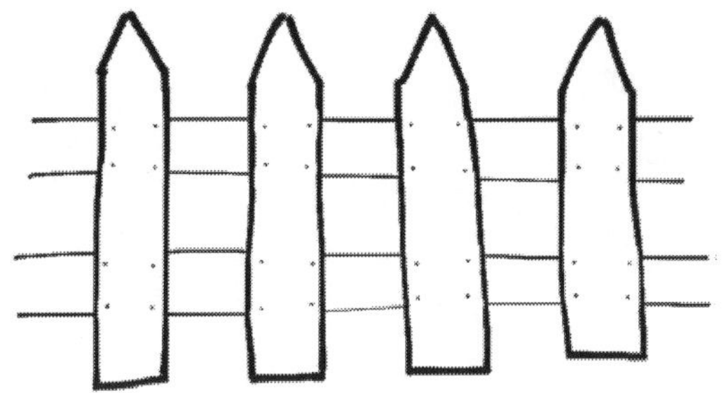

Boundaries

Barrier

Breakthrough

Section

Region

Rural

MOON SUN STARS

Thinking
Thoughts
Dreams
Emotions
Planning Ahead
Imagination

RUBBISH BIN/TRASH

Delete

End

Exclude

Leave Out

Throw Away

BALL OF STRING

String

Complexity

Uncertainty

Sorting Out

Clarity

Tie together

FLAGS AND BUNTING

Celebration

Sign

Announcement

Information

Marketing

CALENDAR

Date
Diary
Today
Planning
Special Event
Deadline

CUP/SAUCER

Coffee or Tea
Break
Refreshment
Cafe
Catering
Product

MEDAL

Success
Reward
Award
Best Practice
Leader
Winner

RULER

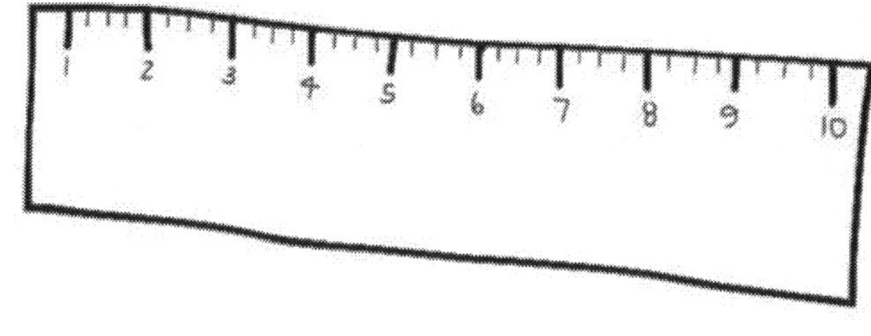

Measure
Evaluation
Metrics
Assess
Quantify
Amount

SIGN

THIS WAY
Direction
Leadership
Strategy
Goal
Target
Information
PRACTICE SKETCHING IT HERE

PENCIL

Pen
Marker
Focus
Sharpen
Write
Document

MAP

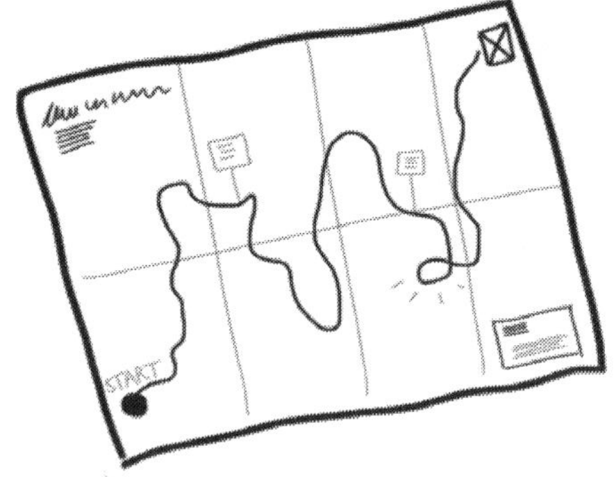

Plan

Strategy

Goal

Journey

Direction

Vision

CHARTS

Research
Data
Surveys
Metrics
Scorecard
Strategy

CITY

Community
Town
Capital
Governance
Marketing
Skyline

IPAD

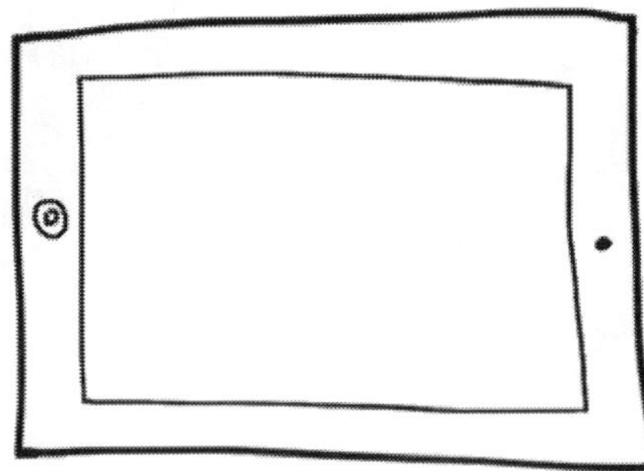

Technology

Mobile Devices

Internet

New Media

Social Media

WINDOW

Idea
Creative
Broad View
Perspective
Insight
Framing

PLAY THE QUICK PICS SKETCH GAME

It's over to you now, to sketch things out. Put your pen to the page and sketch these things. Keep it simple, quick strokes, swift sketches and then move on to the next one! Think about what shape it is…

GHOST	NORTH POLE	THIRD FLOOR
TARGET	SUCCESS	FOR SALE

JELLY	GLASS	ANKLE
TIE	PAPER CLIP	PICTURE FRAME

KEEP PLAYING...

ENVELOPE	COAT HANGER	DOOR MAT
SHIP	RAKE	SHOOTING STAR

BALL & CHAIN	CHRISTMAS TREE	RABBIT EARS
PRICE TAG	NOTICE BOARD	CAMERA

BLANK SPACE FOR YOUR OWN VISUAL MOJO!

PUTTING IT ALL TOGETHER

Now it's time to put the visuals, writing and skills all together!

Way back at the start of Visual Mojo I mentioned how you can turn good into awesome by using words and visuals to **capture**, **convey** and **collaborate**.

And I think that once you know how to **capture** information, ideas and thinking, you can begin to really relax into it and let your Visual Mojo come flooding back and go wild and crazy.

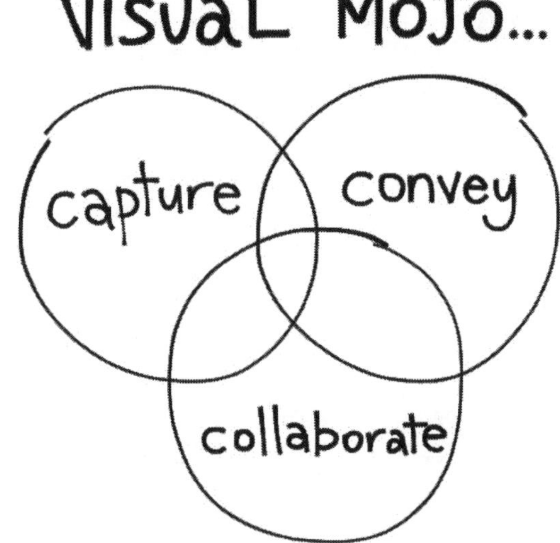

Then the next time you need to **convey** information or ideas, or when you're working with others and need to **collaborate** – whammy, your Visual Mojo will be there because you've already used it to capture!

So before we actually capture some information, ideas and content, a few words, hints and tips about listening.

LISTENING TO CAPTURE

When you're listening out for information, ideas and content, there are some special things to really 'listen out' for.

1. Note the **topic or title** that this information is about. Capture that!

2. If you're listening to a speaker, keep an ear out for their **introduction**. They will often set the scene for the rest of the session, presentation, talk or speech. Those key thoughts or scene setters can be cool to capture too.

3. As they continue on into their talk or presentation, they are likely to **emphasize** some key points. Here's how you'll know that they are key points:

- **Repeating**: speakers will often repeat key phrases, words or ideas. They might deliver them in slightly different ways, but repeating is repeating. Listen out and capture those key words or phrases. As they're speaking, and you're listening, stay alert. See if a visual or icon from Visual Mojo comes to mind that could represent what they're talking about. Capture that!

- **Changing tone**: listen for how the speaker's voice can change tone. It can go from being **deeper** (like a piano keyboard has lower, deeper sounding keys and notes) up to **higher** tones, up the higher end of the piano keyboard.

- **Loudness:** just as voice tone can change, so can the volume. Some speakers almost whisper, as if their volume scale is at level one or two out of ten. Other times, the speaker will get excited, passionate and want to emphasize a point with volume. Their voice volume will go up – the volume level gets turned up and they might be at level seven or eight. Listen for **loudness and softness**.

- **Speed:** speakers will also adjust the speed of their voice. They might **s-l-o-w d-o-w-n** to indicate a point is important or they might **speed up** because it's important.

- **Signposts:** listen for the verbal signposts when you're capturing information. If a speaker or presenter says words like 'firstly' or 'to start off' you know they are … well… starting!

  They may give you other signs that they've got 'three main reasons why' or 'five points to cover'. You'll know they're finishing up when they say 'finally' or 'the key thing I want you to takeaway is' or 'to conclude'.

- **Restating**: speakers give you another chance to capture their key points when they say things like 'in other words' or 'to put it another way' or 'what I'm really saying is'. These are indicators that a key point could be right there, waiting to be captured with Visual Mojo!

4. Listen out for language that shows the **links** between their information.

If they say 'first… second… third', they're showing you how they've broken the information into parts.

If they're using words like 'however' or 'on the other hand' or 'to present another view', you know they've divided the information up into parts that they're contrasting. They might be presenting an alternative or highlighting a problem.

When you hear words like 'especially' or 'most important' or 'most significant' it's a sign they are emphasizing key points.

And if they say words like 'because' or 'so' or 'consequently' or 'as a result of', they're presenting information about cause and effect – the relationship between things.

5. Just as you listen out to the beginning or start, take note of the **summary**, conclusion or wrap-up to ensure you've understood the main points.

Overall when you're listening, think about:

- What is she/he saying?
- What does it mean?
- Where is it leading?
- What are the main ideas they're putting across?
- Is this a story?
- Are these facts from some research?
- How can I use this information?
- What visuals are they talking about?

And because you're using Visual Mojo, leave some space on the page where you're capturing words, pictures and visuals. You can always come back at the end of the talk or during a quiet spot in the talk to embellish, add in more detail or fancy it up!

WHERE ARE YOU AT NOW?

Now you've had some skills practice and got a heap of icons and visuals to use, let's revisit a TED Talk, interview, conversation or other capture opportunity.

Listen to a TED Talk at www.ted.com or listen to an interview or conversation, or read an article. Choose a topic that interests you.

Listen… and start capturing.

TRY OUT YOUR VISUAL MOJO

TRY OUT SOME MORE...

Practice another capture. Listen to a talk, a conversation, a meeting or discussion. Listen… and start capturing.

REVIEW... REFLECT

So how did it go… the latest **capture** part of Visual Mojo?

How did you go with those experiences?

What do you like about your Visual Mojo?

What areas would you like to sharpen up or improve on?

NEXT STEPS – WHAT TO DO NOW...?

Now your Visual Mojo is coming back, here are some suggestions on what you can do next…

- [ ] Just doodle… with lines, shapes, words.
- [ ] Read an article on line or in a newspaper or magazine and capture the key points.
- [ ] Put it out there – don't wait to be 'perfect' before you use it. People will appreciate your Visual Mojo even if you feel you're still developing your skills.
- [ ] Practice at every opportunity – listening to interviews, news reports, reading books or newspaper articles, in workshops or seminars.
- [ ] Share your visual notes with others.
- [ ] Step up in a meeting and start capturing at the whiteboard or flip chart. You'll wow them with the visuals you already know how to sketch out!
- [ ] Next time you have to tell someone something, train or share information, try conveying it with visuals.
- [ ] Read up; see the list of references coming up soon…
- [ ] Build your visual vocabulary and grow your own library of visuals. Try sketching out things you see around you.
- [ ] When a team or group is generating ideas or brainstorming, offer to capture their suggestions using Visual Mojo.
- [ ] When you're studying and learning a new skill, new information or a new concept, capture the key points to help you retain the information.
- [ ] Create a visual 'to do' list. (I like to create a visual shopping list before I head off to the supermarket!)
- [ ] Try using Visual Mojo in meetings that have minutes or notes. They'll be more interesting to read and easier to recall.

THAT JUST ABOUT WRAPS IT UP FOLKS

It's over to you! You have the skills of Visual Mojo – lines, words, shapes, visual images and some listening tips. If you've already put it in to practice a couple of times, you'll start to see how you are improving.

BUT BEFORE YOU GO . . .

Take a couple of minutes to make some commitments here, in this book, on this page. Put a few bullet points here. What will you do LESS of regarding Visual Mojo? What will you do MORE of… what will you keep doing the SAME. You might aim to write less words; or keep the same type of layout on your page; or practice more icons and visuals; or perhaps go back and re-do the Visual Mojo Quick Pics…

LESS	SAME	MORE

HERE ARE SOME I PREPARED EARLIER...

I use Visual Mojo most days of the week:

To capture my ideas

To graphic record at conferences and events

To map out corporate strategies and visions

To help people make sense of big chunks of detail

To cut a way through complexity

To help people hear each other

To see what's really being said

To facilitate a team discussion

To deliver information in workshops, seminars or learning environments

To take notes in meetings.

So over the next few pages are a few of my Visual Mojo captures from early days and more recent times.

Euvin Naidoo TED Talk: On investing in Africa (on a whiteboard in black and orange marker)

See www.ted.com

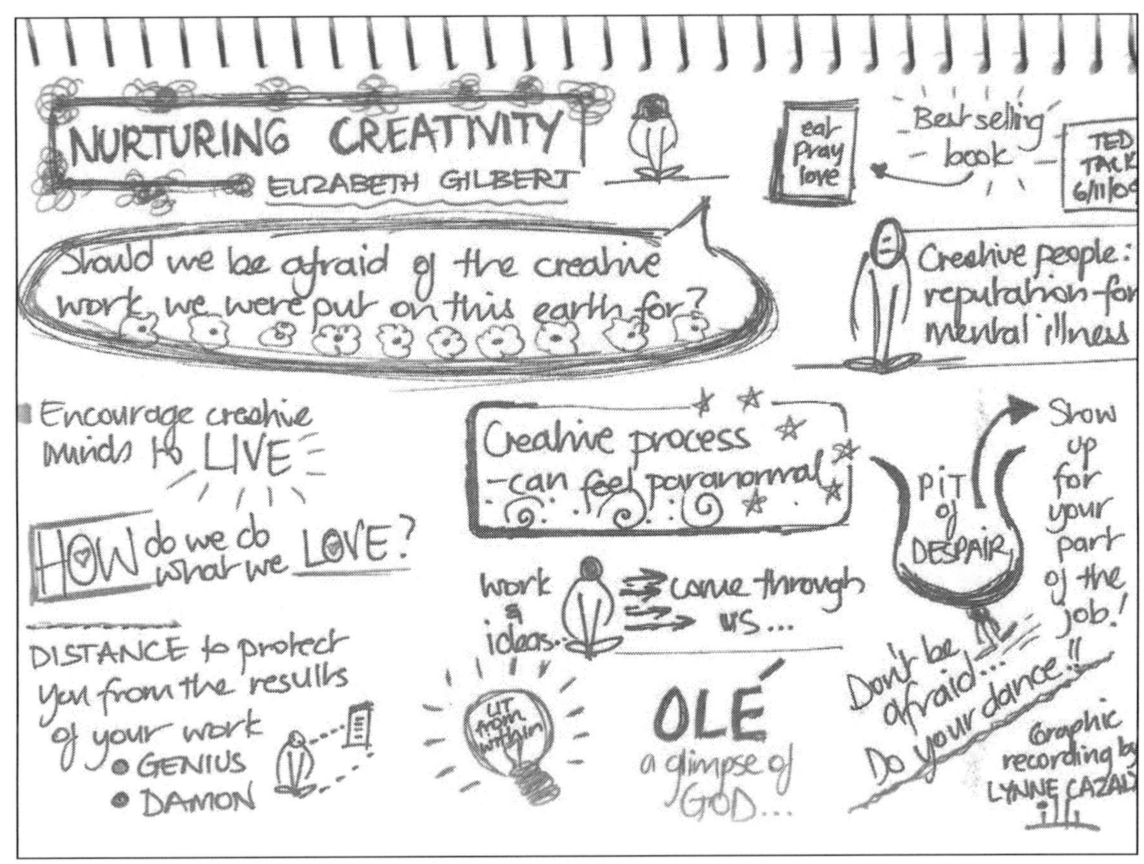

Elizabeth Gilbert's TED Talk: Your elusive creative genius (in an A5 journal in red and black ink)

See www.ted.com

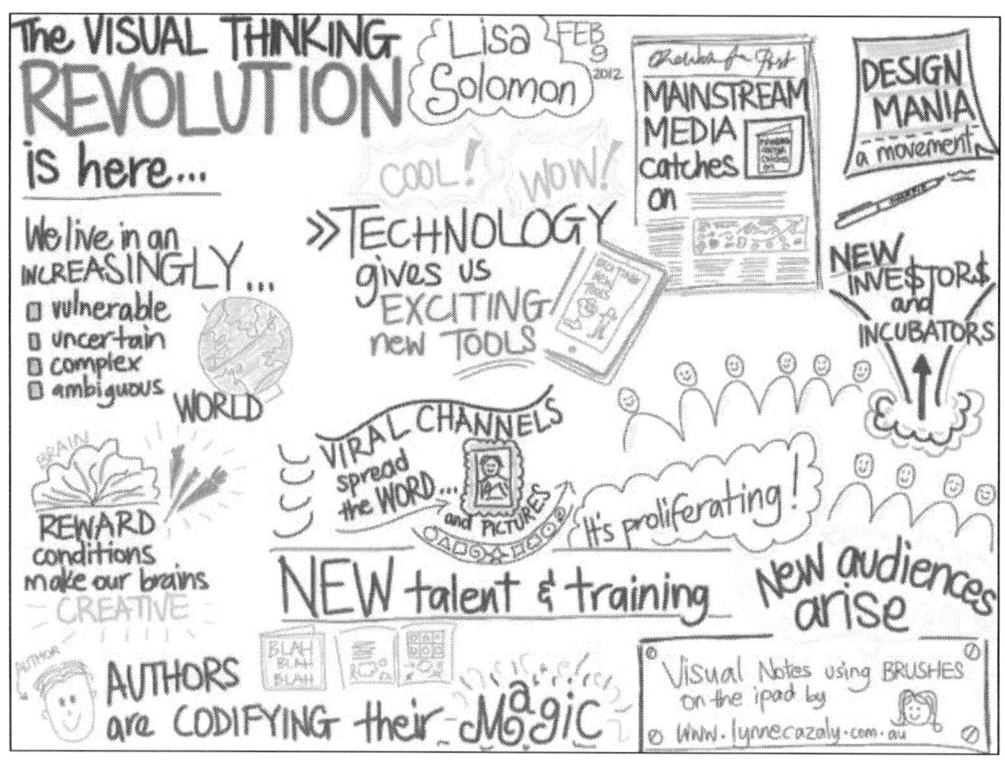

Lisa Solomon's blog article: The Visual Thinking Revolution is here (on the iPad using the Brushes app)

See www.duarte.com/blog/the-visual-thinking-revolution-is-here/

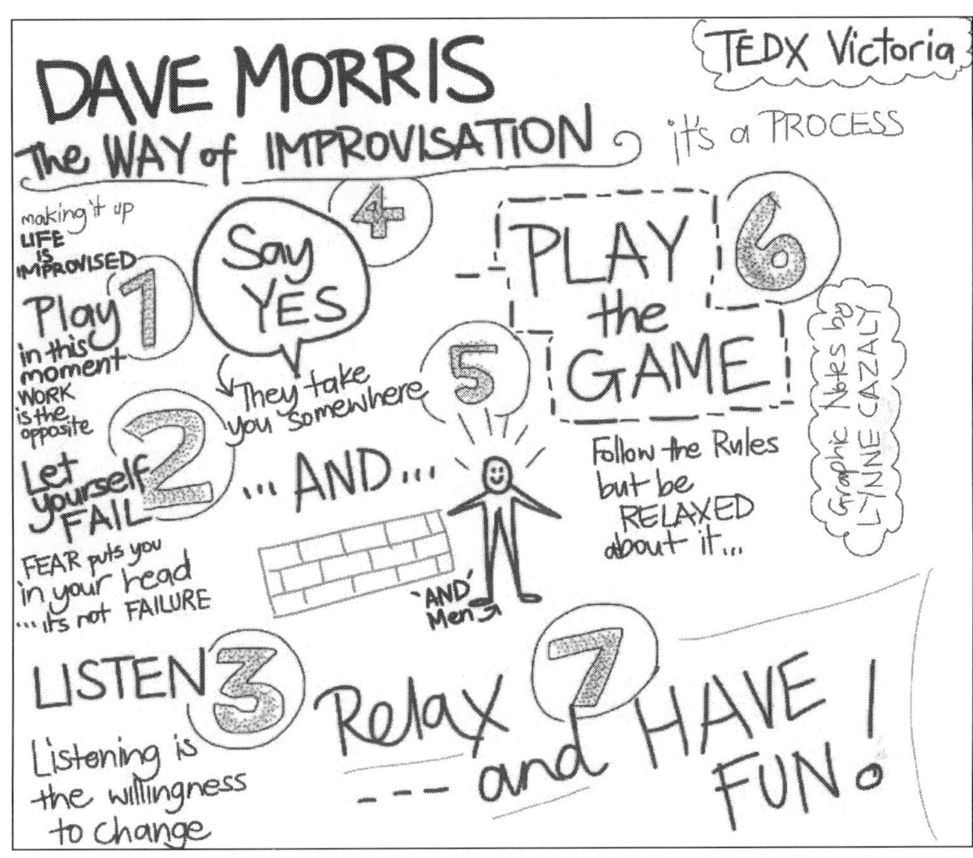

Dave Morris' TED Talk: The way of improvisation (on the iPad using the Brushes app)

See www.ted.com

Seth Godin's Manifesto: Stop Stealing Dreams

I read a few pages of the manifesto each night and took these notes on my Ipad as I read

See www.stopstealingdreams.com

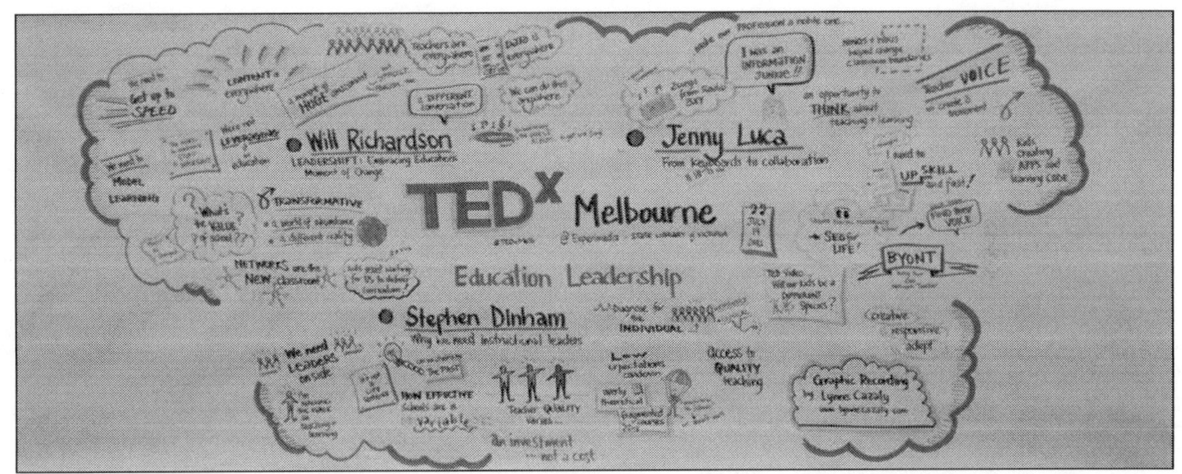

At a TEDx Melbourne event

Jenny Luca, Stephen Dinham and Will Richardson's TED Talks (using a paper wall chart and Neuland markers)

WANT TO SEE MORE?

For more Visual Mojo by Lynne Cazaly please visit her Flickr photostream at:

www.flickr.com/photos/lynnecazaly/

or www.lynnecazaly.com

WANT TO READ MORE?

Agerbeck, Brandy. The graphic facilitator's guide. S.l.: Loosetooth.com, 2012.

Hanks, Kurt, and Larry Belliston. Rapid viz: a new method for the rapid visualization of ideas. Experimental ed. Los Altos, Calif.: W. Kaufmann, 1980.

Kleon, Austin. Steal like an artist: 10 things nobody told you about being creative. New York: Workman Pub. Co., 2012.

Roam, Dan. The back of the napkin: solving problems and selling ideas with pictures. New York: Portfolio, 2008.

Roam, Dan. Blah blah blah: what to do when words don't work. New York: Portfolio/Penguin, 2011.

Rohde, Mike. The sketchnote handbook: the illustrated guide to visual note taking. San Francisco, CA: Peachpit Press, 2013.

Scott, Linda. How to be the best bubble writer in the world ever!. London: Laurence King, 2011.

Sibbet, David. Visual meetings: how graphics, sticky notes, & idea mapping can transform group productivity. Hoboken, N.J.: John Wiley & Sons, 2010.

Sibbet, David. Visual teams: graphic tools for commitment, innovation, & high performance. Hoboken, NJ: John Wiley & Sons, 2011.

Sibbet, David. Visual Leaders. New York: John Wiley & Sons, 2013.

ABOUT THE AUTHOR – LYNNE CAZALY

Lynne Cazaly is a communications specialist.

She's loved words and worked with words all her life. She has consulted, worked and trained people for years about how to write words, strategise with words and communicate with words.

Enough with the words!

In this techo, fast-paced, international world, the words on their own are not enough to communicate effectively. In fact they've become too much for us all to take in.

Lynne helps people engage with each other using words… plus visuals and creative collaborative techniques. When you put these things together, great stuff happens in the world.

She's a great advocate of 'co' – doing things together, with others. And words + visuals help people do this well.

She works with her corporate and community clients as a facilitator, trainer, coach and mentor. She works with organizations as a master facilitator and helps bring clarity to complex projects and situations.

Lynne has trained hundreds of people in how to regain their 'Visual Mojo' when they're leading teams, presenting information, problem solving or leading a workshop or meeting.

She provides training in visual thinking, creative collaboration and innovative leadership, so this book is just like a training program in your hands!

Lynne wants you to take the visual skills you get from Visual Mojo and work with others on your projects, ideas, activities and work.

More information at www.lynnecazaly.com

OH GO ON! PRACTICE SOME MORE...

34829049R00102

Made in the USA
Lexington, KY
20 August 2014